EAST RENFREWSHIRE

MARCO POLO

D1076646

ÁKYNTHOS

...ACA, KEFALONIÁ, LÉFKAS

SERBIA

MNE RKS BULGARIA

Bari MAC.

ITALY ALBANIA

Igoumenitsa TURKEY

Athens

Sicily
(I) Zákynthos

MALTA GREECE

Crete

Mediterranean Sea

LIBYA

www.marco-polo.com

SYMBOLS

INSIDER TIP	Insider Tip
★	Highlight
●●●●	Best of ...
☼	Scenic view
☺	Responsible travel: fair trade principles and the environment respected

PRICE CATEGORIES HOTELS

Expensive	over 100 euros
Moderate	60–100 euros
Budget	under 60 euros

Prices are for two persons in a double room including breakfast, in high season

PRICE CATEGORIES RESTAURANTS

Expensive	over 16 euros
Moderate	12–16 euros
Budget	under 12 euros

Prices are for a meat dish with side dishes, salad and a glass of wine

CONTENTS

Léfkas → p. 52

Zákynthos → p. 64

Trips & Tours → p. 84

Road atlas → p. 114

DID YOU KNOW?

Timeline → p. 12
Sea watermills → p. 43
Books & Films → p. 61
More than a 1000
nests → p. 71
Currency converter → p. 103
Budgeting → p. 105
Weather on Zákynthos
→ p. 106

MAPS IN THE GUIDEBOOK

(116 A1) Page numbers
and coordinates refer to
the road atlas
(0) Site/address located
off the map. Coordinates are
also given for places that are
not marked on the road atlas
Maps of Lefkáda, Zákynthos
Town, Argostóli and Olympia
can be found inside the back
cover

**INSIDE BACK COVER:
PULL-OUT MAP →**

PULL-OUT MAP 〰

(〰 A1) Refers to the
removable pull-out map

The best MARCO POLO Insider Tips

Our top 15 Insider Tips

INSIDER TIP **Healthy eating**
The Polyphemus taverna on Ithaca serves lots of vegetarian and low-fat Greek food → p. 36

INSIDER TIP **Guided hikes**
If you enjoy nature, want to know more about Mediterranean plants and hear all about Odysseus, then take a guided hike across Ithaca with Ester van Zuylen (photo right) → p. 37

INSIDER TIP **In a sea of flowers**
On the terrace of the Kástro taverna on Kefaloniá you can sit below a Venetian castle between countless colourful flowers → p. 47

INSIDER TIP **Traces of the ancient past**
The Archaeological Museum on Léfkas is particularly attractive and there is also information about musical instruments, the monetary history of the island and the ancient art of weaving → p. 54

INSIDER TIP **Special restaurant**
As one of the most unusual restaurants in the Ionian Sea, the Portokáli on Zákynthos serves excellent cuisine in beautiful surroundings, with modern art, and sometimes even with live music → p. 77

INSIDER TIP **Stylish living**
On Zákynthos an old olive press, grain mill and wine cellar has been converted into a very atmospheric hotel, the Archontikó Village. Guests may choose to stay in a variety of charming, well-appointed maisonettes or apartments; the swimming pool is situated in a lush garden full of blooms → p. 80

INSIDER TIP **Dream accommodation**
The name says it all: the small establishment of Dreams on Kefaloniá offers lovely accommodation in one of eight studios with green lawns that stretch all the way down to the beach and its private beach bar → p. 50

BEST OF ...

GREAT PLACES FOR FREE
Discover new places and save money

FOR FREE

● **Discover nature**

In the botanical garden *Cephalonia Botanica* on Kefaloniá you will find yourself alone with the flora of the Ionian Islands, because apart from a few school groups, no one else visits. Information panels have the names of the flowers, herbs, trees and shrubs and you can also find a nice spot for a picnic. Entrance is free → p. 41

● **Be a knight**

The admission-free *Kastro*, above the Livátho Valley on Kefaloniá, looks like a medieval adventure playground for the whole family and offers a fantastic view over the fertile stretch of land to the sea and to the island mountains of Énos → p. 43

● **Noble living**

In the *Lixoúri Museum* you can experience how the rich Kefalonians lived more than a century ago, at no cost. The stately villa's ceiling frescoes alone would be unaffordable today → p. 45

● **Collect some Grecian pitch**

At the *tar springs in Kerí* on Zákynthos visitors can collect a small amount of pitch as it comes out of the ground and take it home as a free souvenir. Best to keep it in a very tight container ... → p. 70

● **Visit those in need of protection**

In the *National Marine Park Exhibition Centre* on Zákynthos, you can learn more about sea turtles (photo) and the fauna of the marine national park. You can also enjoy the ceramic works of art and keep the children busy with arts and crafts → p. 72

● **Liquid gold**

During the winter you can see how olive oil is made at a modern *olive press* in Lithákia on Zákynthos (or hear the explanation throughout the whole year), an olive oil tasting is part of the experience → p. 71

●●●● Dots in guidebook refer to 'Best of ...' tips

● *Regional cuisine*

To unveil the mysteries of Ionian Island cuisine, book an evening cooking course with Vassilikí and Giórgos Balí in the village of *Karavádos* on Kefaloniá. Herbs and other ingredients are gathered from their garden and then enjoyed with other international guests → p. 91

● *Ionian wine*

Wine has been cultivated on all the Ionian Islands for millennia. The white Robóla, which is considered to be typical of the islands, is mainly produced by the *wine cellars* on Kefaloniá. They are open to visitors and also offer free wine tastings → p. 43

● *Unique icons*

Icons are omnipresent in Greece but the Ionian Islands have evolved a distinct form of icon painting developed under the Venetian influence. In the *Zákynthos Museum* (photo) in the island's capital you can see classic Byzantine icons as well as works in the Ionian School typical of the islands → p. 74

● *Hoping for miracles*

The saints play an important role in the life of the islanders, who pray to them for help. The *Church of Saint Dioníssios* in Zákynthos Town is very impressive and pilgrims visit the sarcophagus of the island saint all day long → p. 75

● *Listen to kantádes*

The Zakynthians have a reputation as the Greeks who love to sing. Operatic arias and classical songs are sometimes even heard in tavernas. Everyone sings along when the typical Zakynthian *kantádes* are sung, as it happens every evening in the *Varkaróla Taverna* in Zákynthos Town → p. 80

● *A social enterprise*

Delicious homemade drinks (those that can otherwise only be enjoyed in private households) are produced and served in the *Bell Tower Café* in Argostóli Kefaloniá, an initiative run by people with disabilities. Try their almond juice *soumáda* or plum *vissináda*. Dried herbs, jams and preserved fruit are also sold → p. 47

ONLY IN

BEST OF ...

RAIN

● *Simply dive in*
The rain plays no role when you are under water. In Limní Kerioú on Zákynthos you can book a short introductory dive course at both local *diving schools* → p. 92

● *Explore the underworld*
In the *Drongaráti Cave* (photo) on Kefaloniá, it may constantly be dripping from the ceiling, but nobody gets wet. Over the millennia the water has formed bizarre stalagmites and stalactites → p. 42

● *Ancient dance*
The clay relief in the *Archaeological Museum* of Kefaloniá is proof that the rain dance of the islanders is an ancient tradition: six lovely maidens have been dancing around Pan who is playing his double flute for over 2000 years → p. 40

● *Piety and pomp*
In the *Monastery of Saint Gerássimos* on Kefaloniá you can spend a dry hour when you descend into the old monastery church in the former hermitage and thereafter marvel at the precious interior of the new monastery church → p. 43

● *Make pottery turtles*
It could be a blessing in disguise if it rains on a Tuesday or Saturday. On these days the studio of the ceramicist *Hanne Mi* on Zákynthos is open to the public and you can try to make your own ceramic sea turtle → p. 78

● *Animal parade*
In the private *Helmi's Natural History Museum* on Zákynthos you can explore the animal kingdom without getting wet. Here the flora and fauna animals of the island are gathered in the form of exhibits and fossils → p. 69

RELAX AND CHILL OUT
Take it easy and spoil yourself

● *In British hands*
Locals and tourists alike enjoy the massages and Reiki treatments of the British couple Chris and John Phillips (originally from Bournemouth), whose healing hands work all year long in *Svoronáta* on Kefaloniá, at affordable prices → **p. 49**

● *Like Robinson Crusoe*
At the *Vatsa Club* on Kefaloniá you will feel as if you have been whisked away to a more peaceful world. On the beach next to the river mouth time seems to stand still, the relaxed mood of the regular guests and hosts add to the attractiveness of the hideaway → **p. 50**

● *The good old days*
The laissez-faire feeling of the 1970s can be felt in the *Pub Old House* in Argostóli on Kefaloniá where the host Leftéris is its representative. He gets support from the music stars of that era, the best area for relaxed chats are at the long bar → **p. 49**

● *A day at sea*
You can take a *motor boat* from Nidrí on Léfkas for a relaxed sea trip. While you bask in the sun on the deck, the captain steers the boat along the most spectacular beaches off Léfkas, the most beautiful little harbours on Kefaloniá and even sails into a sea grotto → **p. 90**

● *Enjoy the peace and quiet*
Loúcha on Zákynthos (photo) is one of the most peaceful villages of the Ionian Islands. You can sit under grapevines at one of the *kafenío* and enjoy regional cuisine and fresh spring water, read or play Távli and let the host (who speaks English very well) tell you all about the island → **p. 77**

● *Horse-drawn carriage*
Experience the spruced up little town Zákynthos with a trip in a *horse-drawn carriage*. The best time for this is in the early evening, when the lanterns bathe the old facades in a warm glow → **p. 97**

INTRODUCTION

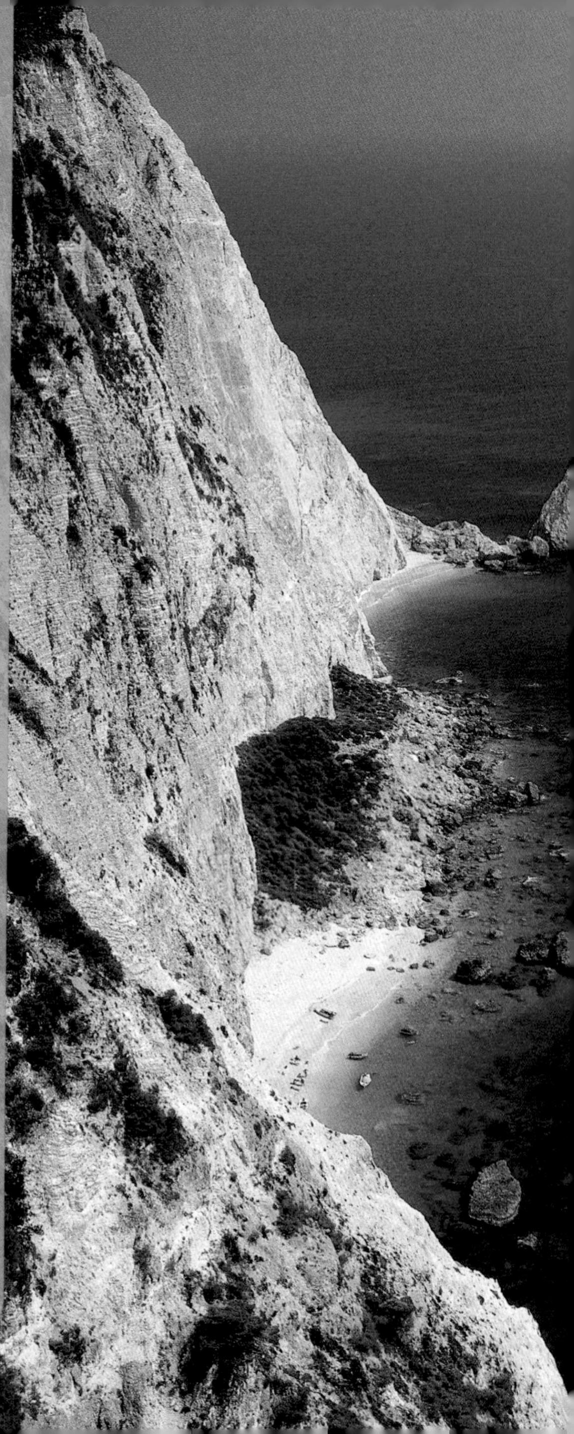

DISCOVER THE IONIAN ISLANDS!

Boats that sail right into blue grottos, secluded coves where the iridescent Ionian Sea shimmers in every conceivable shade of green, turquoise and blue. White cliffs that plunge almost vertically into the sea and olive groves that sweep right to the coast. Picturesque villages, ancient castles, bathing beaches: Zákynthos and its neighbouring islands seem to have been made for holidays. Beautiful whitewashed towns invite you to stroll and narrow, winding roads take you on island expeditions. Two national parks await exploration, old monasteries sit languidly and wine estates invite you for tastings – and the sun shines almost every day during summer.

Off the west coast of Greece, between the south of Albania and the north-west of the Peloponnese, lies a 240km/149mi chain of twelve inhabited islands. Othoní, north

Photo: Steep cliffs on Zákynthos

of Corfu, is closest to Italy and Zákynthos forms the southern end of the chain. Léfkas is only a few kilometres from the Greek mainland and there many small islands off its east coast while Ithaca nestles to the north of Kefaloniá. The straits, with green shores and mountains, are reminiscent of the lovely northern Italian lakes. The islands mostly have impressive cliffs that drop off into the sea which forms fine sandy beaches on Léfkas, Kefaloniá and Zákynthos. The interior of the island is characterised by impressive landscapes of rugged mountain ranges, among the highest on the Greek archipelago.

Unlike many of the Aegean Islands, the Ionian Islands are relatively green. Large areas are covered with ancient olive woods and groves that are dotted with dark, slender cypress trees punctuating the forest of silver leaves that shimmer in the sun. In some places dense pine trees and forests can be found – and way up at

Énos on Kefaloniá there is even a pine forest which has been declared a national park. Little wonder then that the diversity of the landscape attracts those who enjoy the outdoors and hikes. Some visitors want to explore the surprising world that lies beyond the island beaches such as the beautiful stalactite caves on Kefaloniá, the numerous sea caves and grottos on Zákynthos. Naturally most holidaymakers come to enjoy the beaches and the pleasantly warm sea. There are endless stretches of beaches with the finest sand, such as along the Bay of Laganás on Zákynthos or on Kefaloniá's Palíki Peninsula, but there are also sand and pebble beaches where there are crashing waves during rough seas. Many beaches are surrounded by pine forests or olive groves. Sailors, surfers, divers and water sports fans will all find their favourite beach on any of the islands.

In the unspoilt island interior sheep still have the right of way – such as here on Kefaloniá

Corfu (for more detailed information see the Marco Polo 'Corfu' guide) is the most populous and economically the strongest of the Ionian Islands (pop. 103,000) but it is not the only one that is well developed for tourism. During the summer Léfkas and Zákynthos are also filled with more tourists than locals. On Kefaloniá and Ithaca however, tourism plays second fiddle. On both islands agriculture plays the

White sandy beaches and imposing cliffs

more important role and on Kefaloniá, Léfkas and Zákynthos there is also the cultivation of vines and olives. Although there are fishermen everywhere, they cannot even meet the needs of the locals with their catch.

1204
The Venetians provide assistance to the Fourth Crusade to conquer Constantinople. The Ionian Islands are divided among Italian aristocratic families

1386
The Venetians take Corfu, in 1482 Zákynthos, in 1500 Kefaloniá and in 1503 Ithaca. Léfkas falls under Turkish rule in 1467 and is only taken under Venetian rule in 1684

1815–64
The Ionian Islands become an independent republic; albeit a protectorate of the United Kingdom

1864
Unification with Greece

There are no archaeological excavations of regional importance – due to their remote location the Ionian Islands were not an important area during antiquity. In the Middle Ages they (along with the rest of Greece) formed part of Byzantium, and thereafter to Venice. They have the Venetians to thank for the fact that the Ionian Islands – except for Léfkas which is closer to the mainland – were never under Turkish rule, unlike the rest of Greece which was under Ottoman rule for more than 450 years. As a result there are no Turkish-Oriental influences, no mosques or minarets. Instead of wooden bay windows, Venetian influenced arcades and multi storey houses are typical elements of the Ionian architecture. The folk music lacks the distinctive Aegean sound – and even in the visual arts the Ionian Islands have gone their own way. While the rest of Greece fell under the Ottoman rule in the 16th century (with the exception of the Venetian Crete) the artists on the Ionian Islands worked under the influence of Italy, they went to Italy to train and worked in Italian workshops. When Crete came under the Turkish rule during the 17th century, many Cretan artists moved to the Ionian Islands and their work then reflected Western influences: thus the artistic style of the Ionian School was born. The best overview of the school can be seen in the Zákynthos Museum.

> **A unique art style developed on the Ionian Islands**

In addition to Venice, Britain also played a role in the fact that the Ionian Islands differ from the rest of the Greece. Napoleon conquered Venice in 1797 and during that same year he placed the islands under French rule. In the next few years, they were subjected to different rulers – France, Russia and England – until the Congress of Vienna in 1815 when they were declared a British protectorate as the United States of the Ionian Islands. The 49 years in which British Lord High Commissioners treated the islands more as a colony than a protectorate meant that the archipelago were provided with the a good road network and modern water supply to the towns. Despite all the various foreign influences, the Ionian Islands remain a genuine piece of Greece. The islanders repeatedly revolted against foreign rule and supported the rest of Greece (despite a British ban) in their battle for freedom from the Turks in 1821–29. They pushed for the unification of their islands to free Greece and in 1864 Corfu and the other Ionian Islands were finally united with the motherland.

1941–44
The Ionian Islands are invaded by Italian and German troops

1953
Severe earthquake

1967–74
Military dictatorship

1975
Abolishment of the monarchy and establishment of a modern democracy

2004
Summer Olympic Games in Athens

Since 2010
Greece is kept from bankruptcy only through massive aid from the EU and the IMF

During the summer in the popular seaside resorts you will not find the typical Greek lifestyle anymore, there are lots of international influences. In August they are dominated by the Italians and the rest of the summer months by the Dutch, British and Germans. However the towns have a more traditional Greek character – especially the villages in the island interior.

Mediterranean village ensemble in cream tones: Spyridon Square in Lefkáda on Léfkas

If you take a seat at a coffee house on the *platía* the a village then before long you will no longer be a stranger, most of the villagers pass the village square many times a day. Afterwards a stroll through

Very soon you are no longer a stranger

the village will have a different feel to it, by then you will feel almost as if you belong there. The coffee house is the best place to meet the locals and to observe the rhythm of village life. One sees farmers who work the fields with donkeys or mules, children in school uniform, hear the travelling Roma promote their wares over the crackling speakers of their vans, old men having discussions and watch as they play *Távli* (a kind of backgammon), cards or checkers.

To get to know the Greece that is not yet dominated by tourism, you have to go for a walk through the olive groves and spend a leisurely hour in a fishing port. Then you may well be so taken by the real Greece that you might consider leaving your hotel and spending a night in a quiet mountain village.

WHAT'S HOT

1 Hot nights

Nightlife Zákynthos has a vibrant nightlife scene and the party hot spot is the main bar street in Laganás. Here the best DJs in the world spin their tracks in the *Rescue Beach Club (www.rescueclub.net, photo)*, or they cool off after a night of dancing in the unisex shower of the *Cherry Bay Beach Club (www.facebook.com/groups/cherrybaybeachclub)*. Still looking for more? There is also the *Club Zero (www.facebook.com/Zeros ClubZante)* and the *Sizzle Club (www.facebook.com/sizzleclub.zante)* on the main road.

Roll up your sleeves 2

Agritourism Olive harvests, grape harvesting, cheese making: more and more tourists want a holiday where they can pitch in on the farm. On the *Logothétis organic farm (Vassilikí, www.logothetisfarm.gr)* on Léfkas you can do just that – or simply enjoy the nature and home-made specialities and listen to talks about environmental issues. You can also learn something at *Lithiés (Vassilikí, www.lithieshouses.gr, photo)* – such as how honey is collected.

In search of adventure

3

Diving The waters around Zákynthos are like an adventure playground. Caves, wrecks and night dives are popular among experienced divers. *Aquatic Efimia (Aquatic World, 1 Marinou Antipa, Agía Evfimía, Kefaloniá, www.aquatic.gr)* takes night dives to sunken ships. Night dives are also the speciality of the *Nautilus Diving Club (Vassilikí, www.underwater.gr)* where the search for fluorescent sea creatures gets going with underwater cameras. The *Diving Center Turtle Beach (Límni Kerioú, photo)* makes motorcycle fans very happy.

Paddling with a view

4

Stand up paddle surfing The trendy sport from Hawaii has conquered the Grecian islands. If there is not enough wind around Zákynthos and Kefaloniá to surf or sail, water sports enthusiasts can opt for a SUP. Standing on a board and with a long paddle will not only get you out of breath but you also get to see things. This is the popular new way for holidaymakers to explore the coast. *Kefalonia Elements (Argostóli, Kefaloniá, www.kefalonia-elements.com)* helps to get you started and also rents out equipment while the *SUP School (Kefaloniá, www.supschool. gr, photo)* offers guided tours. On Zákynthos the *Peligoni Club (Ágios Nikólaos, Skinari, www.peligoni.com)* offers its guests SUP courses.

With history

5

Culinary The Old Windmill *(Ágios Nikólaos, Navagio, photo)* not only offers breathtaking views, but also typical Greek cuisine in a historic setting. The traditional taverna *Farantou Ladofanaro (Galaro, www.toladofanaro.gr)* is in a converted old olive oil press – and naturally the golden olive oil defines the cuisine of the restaurant. Specialities such as lamb in herb crust and fish in batter is served in the picturesque courtyard in *Pournari (at Orthonies, on the road to Anafonítria)*. The recipes have been handed down from the grandmother and the atmosphere makes you feel as though you are part of a Greek family, enjoying their dinner under the shade.

IN A NUTSHELL

A GÍA, ÁGIOS

Travellers will see the words *Agía, Ágii* und *Ágios* everywhere. They are part of the names of villages and churches, fishing boats and car ferries. *Agía* means saint, *Ágios* is the female form and *Ágíi* the plural of both. Blessed Virgin Mary has a special honorary name, *Panagía,* the Most Holy.

B EACH LIFE

In summer a dip in the sea is almost a daily occurrence for all the islanders. By the end of the summer the locals frequently quiz each other about how often did they went swimming. The quality of the beach does not necessarily play a big role, because most of them would prefer to sit in a taverna after their swim – or go to one of the modern beach bars for a drink and snack served in lounge chairs. Lifeguards are only available on a few of the more popular beaches and then also only during high season.

Although sun loungers and umbrellas are rented out on many of the beaches, you can also just lie on your towel if you prefer. The deck chair rentals and taverna owners usually clean their beaches, and when money is available, so do the local municipalities. There are no private beaches in Greece.

Icons, kiosks and Odysseus: everything you need to know about the Ionian Islands' past and present

BYZANTIUM

The term Byzantium is hardly used anymore – it is the name given to an empire that existed for more than 1000 years and many values and achievements of the ancient world were kept alive well into the late Middle Ages.

The capital of Byzantium, Constantinople, was conquered by the Turks in 1453 and renamed Istanbul. Greeks from Megará near Athens founded the city of Byzantium around 660 BC; Emperor Constantine made it the capital of the empire in AD 330. When Emperor Theodosius divided the empire in AD 395, the city became Constantinople, the centre of the Eastern Roman Empire. While Rome and the Western Roman Empire succumbed to attacks by Visigoths, Vandals and Huns, the Byzantine Emperor retained

Practical solution: ripe olives are collected with nets

and expanded the empire. Under Emperor Justinian I (AD 527–65) the empire extended to Italy, North Africa and far into Asia Minor. The Ionian Islands were still a part of the empire well into the early 12th century.

EARTHQUAKES

Mild earthquakes are common on the Ionian Islands. However, a catastrophic earthquake destroyed the southern islands on the 9–12 August 1953. This destroyed 94 per cent of the homes on Zákynthos, 91 per cent on Kefaloniá and 70 per cent on Ithaca. That is why so few villages on these islands have any traditional architecture.

FAUNA

Cats and dogs are the animals that holidaymakers are most likely to encounter. Wild mammals have become rare. There are reportedly still rabbits, foxes, martens, hedgehogs and weasels. The bird life is richer and one can see magpies and golden orioles, hoopoes and jays, cuckoos, swallows and the Little Owl. In the more isolated mountain regions you can also still see buzzards and hawks, and herons along the flat coastal regions.

You may occasionally encounter a snake on hikes. The only one that is venomous is the sand viper; the non-venomous ones include the whip snake and Montpellier snake. Tortoises are common, scorpions rare. The sea has been exploited by over fishing and dynamite fishing, raising the price of fish. Dolphins are occasionally seen, there has never been a shark encounter in these waters.

FINANCIAL CRISIS

The crisis that became apparent in 2010 is far more than just an economic and financial crisis. It has touched every aspect of Greek society and forced changes in all reaches of life. Many taxes have been increased while wages, pensions and social benefits have been reduced. Many of the population are now impoverished and the social network inadequate.

It may take many years for Greece to recover. The islands are especially dependant on tourism; the islanders are very aware of this and will therefore do everything to ensure that the tourists enjoy their holiday.

FLORA

Olive trees and cypresses are the most distinctive trees of the Ionian Islands. Along rivers there are mighty plane trees; eucalyptus is the popular tree along avenues, and the sandy sea shores are home to the robust tamarisk. Large uncultivated areas are occupied by the *phrygana*, a mixed vegetation of broom, sage, butterfly lavender, thyme, oregano and dwarf juniper.

The dark native Kefaloniá pine grows along the Énos massif. In addition to the well-known fruit varieties, medlars are also grown in gardens; grapes thrive everywhere, in particular on Zákynthos and Kefaloniá.

HUNTING

Many Greek men are passionate hunters. According to one estimate by the Greek animal welfare society almost 400,000 men go hunting annually, many of them illegally. Hunting protection laws are in place, but are rarely observed. Early each year, hunters from all over the country meet on Zákynthos. On this island alone there are 13,000 officially registered hunting rifles are, but in reality the number is closer to 30,000.

ICONS

In the Orthodox Church icons are the representations of saints and biblical events on panel paintings. They are found in all the churches, but also in private homes and in vehicles. Icons are quite different from the religious images in our churches. They are the 'gates to heaven' and they bring the saints into the home, making them ever present. They enjoy a lot of respect and are kissed, decorated with precious metals, embroidered curtains, precious stones, rings and watches. Icons are considered as the consulates of heaven on earth and are treated as if they were the saints themselves.

KIOSKS

Kiosks or *períptero* (the Greek singular) are situated in every square and in the towns and villages at the larger intersections. They are usually open from early morning until late at night and sell everything that might be needed urgently: cigarettes and razor blades, toothbrushes and combs, single aspirins, condoms and much more.

KOMBOLÓI

Elderly men in particular like to play with a *kombolói*, a chain similar to a rosary. However, it has no religious significance, but only serves as a way to pass the time. The Greeks probably modified theirs from the Turkish prayer beads; the Greek worry beads always have an uneven number usually 13 or 17.

LOTTERY TICKET SELLERS

Lottery ticket sellers are as much a part of the Greek street scene as Orthodox priests and kiosks. Two lottery types are available: scratch cards with the possibility of winning instantly and tickets for the state lottery, where the numbers are drawn on Mondays.

ODYSSEUS

Ithaca is regarded as the home of Odysseus, the hero of 'The Odyssey', the famous 2700 year old epic which is attributed to the legendary poet and singer Homer. The epic involves Odysseus' (the King of Ithaca) participation in the Trojan War, which Homer described in his other epic 'The Iliad'. After the end of the war, the hero and his companions set sail for Ithaca. The journey home took ten years and Odysseus was the only one to survive. First Odysseus sailed with his men to the Thracian town of Ismaros which they then plundered. They set sail again and were blown off course to the land of the lotus eaters where his companions enjoyed some lotus plants (which put them in a dream state) and Odysseus was then compelled to force them back on board. Things got worse when they landed on an island of Cyclopes; one of them, Polythemus, later devoured two of his men. Then they visited Aeolus a mortal who had control of the winds who gave Odysseus a bag in which he could capture all the adverse winds except for the wind that blew towards Ithaca. But when Ithaca was finally in sight, his curious companions opened the bag and the fleet was driven by a violent storm to the Laistrygonians. They destroyed all the ships save for that of Odysseus and devoured many of the Ithacans. Those remaining went with their king to the island of the sorceress

Immortalised by Homer: a bust of Odysseus in Stavrós on Ithaca

Circe, who turned many of the men into swine, but at the urging of Odysseus she once again made them human.

Next they survived the alluring song of the sirens — Odysseus plugged wax in their ears and tied himself to the mast to avoid temptation — only to have the six-headed monster Scylla kill six of his men. Then on the island of Trinacria, Zeus killed his remaining companions after they ate the sacred cows of the sun god Helios. Odysseus sailed away alone and came to the nymph Calypso, who lovingly held him captive for seven years. After which she was ready to let him go. Odysseus left on a raft and a storm washed him ashore on Corfu. The rulers for the local Phaeacians gave him a boat with which he finally returned to his home after his ten year odyssey.

RENEWABLE ENERGY

Greece has wind and sun in abundance yet both are not used nearly enough for energy production. Solar panels are widely used to heat water in private households and hotels. Photovoltaic systems for energy production, which was pioneered for Greece on Crete, are still absent on the Ionian Islands.

The generation of electricity from wind power is slightly better. On Kefaloniá three wind parks already feed about 50 megawatt of electrify annually into the power grid. On the other island wind turbines — largely funded by the EU — also add to the reduction of the petroleum products in the mostly outdated island power plants.

RELIGION

Almost all Greeks are Greek Orthodox Christians and those in the countryside are particularly pious.

For tourists the churches and many small chapels draw attention, because they look so different. Many are built in the Byzantine style with a dome and a floor plan in a cruciform; others follow the Italianate style with hall-like churches and high free-standing bell towers. However, none have the statues, confessionals boxes or fonts that you find in Roman Catholic churches.

You will see Orthodox priests all over the Ionian Islands. They always wear long, dark robes, have full beards and a hat under which one or more long braids hang out. Orthodox priests are allowed to marry before their ordination and often have large families. They are paid by the state.

Orthodox Church services often last two to three hours. Only a few worshippers hold out that long so there is a constant coming and going and people often even chat amongst themselves during the service. Its main feature is the antiphonal singing of the daily liturgy which is celebrated by priests and some laity. An important ritual in the Greek Church is the kissing of the icons.

Orthodox Christians do not recognise the Pope as the head of Christianity. The schism in the church came about in 1054, because the Orthodox believe that the Holy Spirit only emanated from the Father, while the 'papists' believed that it also emanates from the Father and the Son.

WASTE DISPOSAL

The waste generated on the island has to be disposed of almost entirely on the island. There are no incinerators and the waste is either burned out in the open air or turned into the soil. Recycling is still in its infancy, because the further processing of separated materials must be done on the mainland, with the added cost of transport costs. This is also the main reason why there is still no refund system for bottles and cans in Greece.

FOOD & DRINK

Greek restaurants and tavernas are not a paradise for gourmets. You will search in vain here for gourmet restaurants such as those found in France and Italy. Yet while Greek cuisine has remained down to earth and unpretentious it is still nonetheless very tasty and this is because the Greeks value good, fresh regional ingredients.

The choice of restaurants and taverna on the island is huge. Many open at 9am and serve full English breakfasts and various omelettes.

The majority of Greek restaurants stay open continuously, serving guests from noon until midnight. For those just want-ing a snack, there is a growing number of modern American style snack bars, but also numerous small barbeque stalls and bakeries. Many of them sell different types of *píttes*, puff pastries with various fillings. *Spanakópitta*, filled with spinach, *tirópitta* with goat cheese, and the *loukanikópitta* with sausage. A sweet version from north-ern Greece is *bougátsa*, which is filled with a light semolina pudding and dusted with powdered sugar.

TAVERNA

A taverna is a traditional eatery that is more informal than a modern Western

Dine like the Greeks: companionship, atmosphere and ambience are more important in Greece than sophisticated cuisine

restaurant. Real tavernas are always simply furnished with wood or metal tables, usually covered with plastic covers or tablecloths. To keep the tabletop clean, the waiter will cover it with a piece of paper. Once done, he will immediately return with a basket of bread – for which you must pay – some paper serviettes and some cheap metal cutlery. You will need to go through to the kitchen (or look on

the hot plate) to see what is on offer or you can ask the waiter for his recommendations.

In restaurants the locals are hardly ever handed menus as they say nothing about the quality of the dishes but there are written menus specially for foreigners. Everyone at the table orders several dishes and the waiter then brings them all to the table simultaneously. The

LOCAL SPECIALITIES

▶ **békri mesé** – a type of pork stew with peppers in a lightly spicy sauce
▶ **bourdéto** – fish or meat (rarely) dish in a spicy tomato sauce with onion, garlic and red pepper. As appetizer mostly prepared with *galéo* (dogfish), as main dish with *skórpios* (scorpion fish) or *pastanáka* (stingray)
▶ **briám** – ratatouille
▶ **chtapódi ksidáto** – octopus pickled in vinegar and oil (photo left)
▶ **fasoláda** – bean soup
▶ **jemistés** – peppers stuffed with rice, minced meat, tomatoes and aubergines
▶ **jouvétsi** – stew that is baked in a clay pot – beef with rice shaped pasta, topped with grilled cheese
▶ **karidópitta** – walnut cake (photo right)
▶ **kléftiko** – roast lamb or goat meat with potatoes
▶ **kreatópitta** – meat baked in puff pastry

▶ **láchanodolmádes** – small cabbage rolls with lemon egg sauce
▶ **loukanikó pita** – spicy pork sausage in pita bread
▶ **márides** – crispy fried sardines, eaten with skin and bones, head and tail
▶ **pastitsáda** – pot roast in a tomato sauce served with noodles
▶ **patsária** – beetroot salad
▶ **revithókeftédes** – chickpea fritters, usually served with a yoghurt dip
▶ **rewáni** – semolina cake
▶ **riganáda** – toasted bread topped with feta, tomatoes, olives and oregano
▶ **savóro** – marinated sardines with currants, served hot or cold
▶ **sofríto** – veal slowly cooked in garlic, white wine sauce
▶ **stifádo** – usually beef (some-times rabbit) stew with vegetables in a tomato sauce flavoured with cinnamon

Greeks do not follow a specific order or even a menu composition. Appetizers, salads and main dishes (whether hot or cold) are all placed on the table at the same time. If you want to avoid this, you should order every course separately. All the dishes are placed in the centre of the table so that everyone can help themselves. The wine is poured into small glasses, and everyone toasts each other with *'Stin ijía mas'* – to our health!

Authenic tavernas usually only serve fruit for dessert, and coffee is rarely available. The bill is issued for the entire table, however, in recent years tavernas have started to allow foreigners to pay for their meals separately. Seafood and fresh fish are often calculated according to weight, so the price on the menu is often the price per kilogram. In order to avoid any unpleasant surprises, it is best to be present while the produce is weighed so that you can immediately ask the price.

OUZERÍ AND KAFENÍON

Traditional Greek restaurants are also *ouzeríes* – a place for locals to drink small carafes of the national drink *oúzo*. *Oúzo* is an anise liquor served with small dishes of octopus, fish and meat dishes, snails, eggs, biscuits, bread, salads or simply just olives, cucumbers and tomatoes; in contrast to other eateries here you order a little bit of everything. You can also let the host decide and simply order *pikilía* and *mezédes* (mixed hors-d'œuvres).

Greek coffee houses are the meeting place of the local men. In the tourist centres they are found either between Western style bars and cafés or out in the suburbs, but in the villages the *kafeníon* is still the centre of social life. There is no obligation to eat or drink so you will often see full *kafenía*, where no one is drinking. The local sit together and discuss God, the world and the Greek politics, or play *Távli*, checkers or cards.

If you order coffee you have to specify exactly how you want it. When Greek coffee is made, the water, the coffee and sugar are all boiled up together. *Kafé ellinikó* comes in many variations: *skétto* (without sugar); *métrio* (with a little sugar); *glikó* (with lots of sugar) and *dipló* (a double). Instant coffee is generally ordered as *neskafé* – either *sestó* (hot) or *frappé* (cold) and it is always best say how sweet you want it.

Fresh appetizers, olives and a glass of wine – this is Greece!

The younger Greeks especially drink *freddo capuccino* or *freddo espresso*, both of which are served in large glasses with lots of ice cubes. During the colder seasons or in the evening they also drink a *rakómelo*, warm raki sweetened with honey and spices.

SHOPPING

The souvenir shops in the cities and seaside resorts often have mass produced wares, which are at best produced on the Greek mainland. It is a better option to buy from the island artisans themselves or to shop in the small shops of the agricultural co-operatives. The souvenir shops and the supermarkets in the resorts are usually open daily from 10am until 10pm/11pm during the summer months. In the cities, supermarkets and shops are closed on Saturday afternoon and Sundays. Many retail outlets also close on Tuesday and Thursday afternoons and have a long afternoon break from 1:30pm to 5pm.

ALMONDS

The Palíki Peninsula on Kefaloniá is famous for its almond specialities: *mándoles* (roasted) and *barboulé* (caramelised) almonds. No visitor leaves Zákynthos without *pastélli*, sweet sesame and honey bars, or *mandoláto*, soft nougat.

CERAMICS

Ceramics from all over Greece (including copies of ancient painted vases) are offered in many shops. The best ceramicist on the island is the Norwegian Hanne Mi, who also offers ceramic courses in her studio/showroom on the Skopós Peninsula on Zákynthos.

JEWELLERY

There are numerous jewellery shops on Zákynthos. The jewellery is slightly cheaper than what you would pay elsewhere in Europe. Be sure to always check the quality though! There is no guarantee that it is produced in Greece as most jewellers buy from wholesalers and trade fairs all over Europe.

MUSIC

Whether it is the traditional *kantádes* or the rock and pop sounds of the Greek charts – music shops in the cities stock all on the local CDs.

OLIVE OIL

The best Greek olive oil is available in all

Shopping along the roadside: honey, wine and olive oil – agricultural products are typical of the Ionian Islands

the island towns. However, due to airline regulations for the transport of liquids, you can only legally be able to take it with you if you buy it at the airport after passing through the security checkpoint. Transporting it in a checked-in bag is not allowed due to the flammability of the oil! There is no restriction for taking olive oil soap or olives.

OLIVE WOOD

Olive wood carvings, including plates, salad servers, bread boards and bowls, are quite rare and also relatively expensive, because the wood has to dry for ten years before it can be processed.

PERFUME

On Kefaloniá and Zákynthos every small business makes eau de toilette. The la-

bels are not very fancy, but the scent is pleasant and not available outside of Greece.

TURTLES

Turtles in the form of plush toys, plastic animals and in ceramics are available on the islands, especially on Zákynthos. In contrast to real turtle shells, they may be taken home.

WINE AND SPIRITS

There is a good selection of Greek wines in the speciality *Cáva* shops in the towns, and on Zákynthos, Kefaloniá and Léfkas you can also visit wineries and buy wine directly. Lefkáda has a shop that sells liqueurs, brandy and oúzo still produced by themselves, sometimes also available straight from the barrel.

THE PERFECT ROUTE

LOVELY ZÁKYNTHOS

From the international ferry port of Pátras the trip goes 70km/43mi to the small port of ① *Killíni* → p. 81. From there the car ferries cross to ② *Zákynthos Town* → p. 74. With its museums and spacious squares filled with street cafés, the town itself is worth a day's visit. You can spend another day on the Skopós Peninsula with its National Park Exhibition Centre and the lovely Gerákas Beach as well as the beautiful beaches around the Gulf of Laganás. On the way back you can also pay a visit to Macherádo with its typical island church. From the hamlet of ③ *Ágios Nikólaos* → p. 67 (photo left) you can cross to Pessáda on Kefaloniá during midsummer. If the ferry is not running, you will first need to return to Pátras via Killíni and from there take the ferry to ④ *Póros* → p. 46 on Kefaloniá.

THE LARGEST OF THEM ALL

From ⑤ *Pessáda* → p. 51 you can stop at the Monastery of Ágios Andréas and then the Kástro Ágios Geórgios which has a lovely view of the island's capital ⑥ *Argostóli* → p. 40. It is a particular good place to explore the island from. A ferry leaves several times a day to ⑦ *Lixoúri* → p. 45 with its beautiful beaches on the southern coast of the Palíki Peninsula. Two full-day tours also lead to the north and the south of the island *(see p. 86/87)*. From ⑧ *Sámi* → p. 46 with its remains of an ancient city and the Melissáni Cave (photo right), which you can explore by boat, you can head to Vathí on Ithaca, the fabled island of the mythical hero.

ON ODYSSEUS' ISLAND

You can spend a whole day in the island capital ⑨ *Vathí* → p. 35 with short walks to some of the locations supposedly from 'The Odyssey', and short boat trips to tiny beaches. In the interior of the island the route leads via the Monastery of Katharón and the village church of Anogí (worth a visit) to *Kióni* → p. 34, the most beautiful village on the island which is in the north. Here you can even try your hand as a captain and rent a motor boat. From the neighbouring village of ⑪ *Fríkes* → p. 34 small car ferries travel to Vassilikí in the south of Léfkas.

Experience the many facets of the Ionian Islands when you go island-hopping between Léfkas and Zákynthos from Pátras to Préveza

WHITE ROCKS & LONG BEACHES

Just west of ⑫ *Vassilikí* → p. 57 the Lefkáta Peninsula, with its characteristic white rocks, stretches out to the south. Its sandy beaches under high cliffs are some of the most attractive in the whole country. The island capital ⑬ *Lefkáda* → p. 55 is ideal for a stroll and museum visits, while the Ionian Sea here offers some of the best surf and kite spots. The main holiday resort of the island is the port town ⑭ *Nidrí* → p. 56, where various boat excursions are available throughout the season.

ISOLATED ISLANDS

One of the boat trips is to ⑮ *Skórpios* → p. 63, the private island of the once world famous ship owner Aristotle Onassis and his wife Jacqueline Kennedy. However, only the beach is accessible to the general public. Occasionally, excursion boats also travel to the inhabited – yet incredibly quiet and peaceful – islands of ⑯ *Kálamos* → p. 62 and ⑰ *Kastós* → p. 62, which are so isolated that they are unknown even to Greeks. Several times a day small car ferries travel to the island of ⑱ *Meganísi* → p. 62, offshore of Léfkas, with its three villages which you can comfortably explore on foot. At the end of your tour you can return from Lefkáda via a causeway to the mainland and through a tunnel to the village ⑲ *Préveza* → p. 63 and from there you can drive 85km/53mi to the international ferry port of Igoumenítsa, from where the large car ferries depart several times a day for Italy.

1200km/746mi.
Driving time: 30 hours without ferry crossings.
Recommended duration: 12–14 days.
Detailed map of the route on the back cover, in the road atlas and the pull-out map

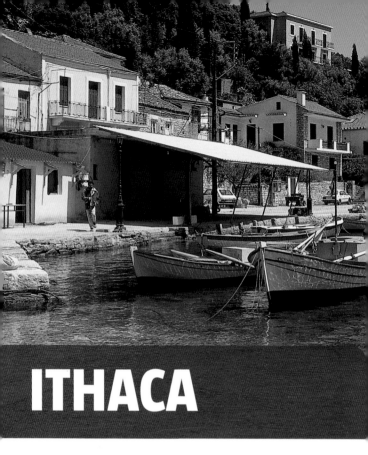

ITHACA

The island of the hero Odysseus, known locally as Thiáki (Ithaca to us), is off the eastern coast of Kefaloniá, from which it is separated only by a narrow inlet.

Ithaca (pop. 3200) is 24km/15mi long and 6km/3.7mi wide; the northern and southern parts of the island are connected by a 600m wide isthmus. When driving along the scenic roads of the island you will have fascinating views of bays and coastline. Most of the villages are located in the hilly, fertile northern part of the island. The villages are increasingly becoming depopulated as fewer young people are willing to accept the low wages and

hard labour of the agriculture and fishing industries. Thus the main area of the island now lies in the south, in the island capital of *Vathí*, and the nearby mountain village of *Perachóri*.

It is certain that Ithaca was populated during the times of the Trojan War around 1200 BC. Whether the island really had a king named Odysseus, is doubtful. The Ithacans themselves believe the myth – and they also try to encourage tourists in this belief. As a result there are numerous places on the island – springs, beaches and caves – that are linked to 'The Odyssey'. Even if these spots are just myths and legends are not historically

Photo: Boats on the Kióni waterfront

Tourists are an unusual sight in the former Kingdom of Odysseus – tourism plays a minor role on Ithaca

real, the beautiful surroundings make the walk there is worth it.

SIGHTSEEING

AETÓS (119 E3) (*∅ D9*)

The ancient city Alalkoméne was once situated on the slope of the 380m/1246ft mountain south-west of Vathí. It was settled from about 1400 BC to Roman times.

On the summit there are some well preserved archaeological ruins with cisterns and a part of the wall of the Acropolis that dates from the 5th century BC. On the pass between the eastern and western coast, where the road that leads from Vathí to the ferry terminal and the overcrowded (during summer) Bay of Pisoaetós, one can still see several large hewn stones from a Hellenistic tower.

The maquis covered ruins of the medieval island capital Perachóri

ANOGÍ ★ ☀ (119 E2) (*ØD8*)

The small mountain village lies about 500m/1640ft high on a plateau strewn with bizarre boulders, some as large as 8m/26ft. On the main road is Anogí's church which is dedicated to the Assumption of the Virgin Mary with campanile and well preserved frescoes dating back to 1670. *The key is in the kafeníon next door.*

ARCHAEOLOGICAL MUSEUM
(119 F3) (*ØD9*)

On display are finds from Alalkoméne, on the slope of Mount Aetós, such as ceramic votives from the Doric sanctuary of Apollo. *Tue–Sat 8.30am–3pm | free admission | Vathí*

ARETHOÚSA SPRING ★ ☀
(119 F4) (*ØE10*)

A beautiful 90 minute hike leads from Vathí to the spring at the base of a steep rock face on the south-east coast of the island. It is here that Eumaeus, Odysseus' swineherd, brought his masters pigs to drink. From the port, follow the 'Arethoúsa

Spring' signposts through the town and then continue on the narrow asphalt road until you reach a sign where the narrow footpath to the spring begins.

DEXIÁ BAY (119 E3) (*ØD9*)

Legend has it that the bay with the small pebble beach is the Homeric Bay of Forkinos, where Odysseus returned from Corfu.

KIÓNI ★ (119 E1–2) (*ØD8*)

Kióni is regarded as one of the most beautiful places on the island. The village lies at the end of a bay surrounded by olive and cypress trees. Here you can rent motor boats and head out to some picturesque bays: on foot or by boat you can reach several small pebble beaches in just a few minutes. In summer ferries connect the neighbouring village of *Fríkes* to Léfkas.

MONASTERY OF KATHARÓN ☀
(119 E2) (*ØD9*)

The monastery lies at 556m/1824ft and its freestanding bell tower has the most

amazing view over large parts of the island.
Mon–Fri, 8am–8.30pm

NAUTICAL AND FOLK MUSEUM
(119 F3) *(ᗰ D9)*
Small local museum in a converted power station. Because Ithaca has been a seafaring island since the time of Odysseus, many of the displays reference the sea. *Typically 9.30am–1.30pm and 6pm–9pm | admission 1.50 euro | Vathí*

GROTTO OF THE NYMPHS
(119 E3) *(ᗰ D9)*
After his successful return to Ithaca, Odysseus left his belongings in the care of the nymphs – mythical creatures that lived in a small cave above Dexiá Bay. Archaeologists are currently excavating the cave (the ceiling caved in during an earthquake in 373 BC) and have found several small finds. *Closed to the public until further notice.*

PERACHÓRI ☆ (119 E3) *(ᗰ D9)*
Only 2km/1.2mi above Vathí at an altitude of 300m/1863ft is the island's largest village (pop. 500). Between the houses on the slopes, there are terraced vineyards and olive groves; the view of the harbour bay is extraordinarily beautiful. Unfortunately there is a lack of appealing tavernas. Several ruins testify to a medieval settlement in the area. Right at the lower village entrance, on the left side of the road, are the remains of a Venetian house and a church, where the remains of some frescoes can still be seen. In the village centre a sign points the way through olive groves to the ruins of St John's church with some more frescoes.

STAVRÓS ★ (119 E2) *(ᗰ D8)*
The largest village in the north of the island (pop. 350) is situated on a mountain ridge, with views of both the east and the west coast of Ithaca. On the village square there is a bust of Odysseus, whose palace was apparently found by an archaeologist in the hamlet of Pelikáta. A cul-de-sac leads you down to the bay of *Pólis*. In the coastal plains traces of an ancient stadium have been found; on the mountain ridge on the other side of the bay, there are also the remains of some ancient walls.

VATHÍ (119 F3) *(ᗰ D9)*
The island's capital (pop. 2000) is a tranquil town with no significant sights. It lies at the inner end of a long fjord-like bay, which winds its way to the sea. It can get quite lively at night in the cafés along the waterfront, which gives one the feeling of sitting on the shores of a large lake. A villa in the harbour designed by German architect Ernst Miller prior to 1953 is now a café bar; the majority of houses in the town were destroyed by the earthquake, including the quarantine station dating

★ **Anogí**
Mountain village, nestled between bizarre boulders, with a church decorated with frescoes → p. 34

★ **Arethoúsa Spring**
Hike through wild natural beauty to a legend → p. 34

★ **Kióni**
The most picturesque village of the island is virtually free of cars → p. 34

★ **Stavrós**
In every good taverna one wonders whether this could have been where Odysseus' palace once stood → p. 35

MARCO POLO HIGHLIGHTS

back to the 19th century on the islet of *Lazaretto*. You can swim to the islet and excursion boats also make trips to the short gravel beaches on the other side of the bay.

FOOD & DRINK

GREGORY'S (119 F3) (*ω D9*)
A well-established taverna directly on the sea, try their marinated fish *savóro*. *Vathí | at the northern end of the harbour | Moderate*

KALKÁNIS (119 F3) (*ω D9*)
A family run taverna with a large selection of dishes, their roast lamb *kléftiko* and the *octopus stifádo* (octopus and onion stew) are both delicious. *Vathí | south just behind the Platía | Budget*

KANTOÚNI (119 F3) (*ω D9*)
Pleasant taverna on the waterfront with a small terrace at the back. *Vathí | Odós Ploiárchou Georg. Gratsoú | Moderate*

LOW BUDGET

▶ Although the ferry trip from Sámi (Kefaloniá) to Pisoaétos is cheaper than the one to Vathí, no buses go to the other island towns from Pisoaétos. So it is better to book a passage to Vathí for those who are not travelling with their own vehicle.

▶ *Níkos* is the cheapest taverna in the island's capital of Vathí and even though it is not near the waterfront, it is still the popular choice of many local regulars. The menu has mostly grilled food and salads, main courses start at about 5 euros.

INSIDER TIP POLYPHEMUS
(119 E2) (*ω D8*)
This restaurant in an old Venetian style building has a beautiful garden and serves traditional dishes, with many options for vegetarians. *Stavrós | on the road to Anogí | Budget*

SIRÍNES (119 F3) (*ω D9*)
Great selection, very tasty roast pork. *Evenings only | Vathí | in the alley parallel to the waterfront promenade | Expensive*

SHOPPING

ELPINÓR
(119 F3) (*ω D9*)
Authentic shop on the waterfront with ship pictures, bric-a-brac, painted pebbles and jewellery. *Vathí | Paralía 160*

SPORTS & BEACHES

INSIDER TIP ÁGIOS IOÁNNIS BEACH
(119 E2) (*ω D9*)
100m/328ft long, 15m/50ft wide isolated pebble beach without a taverna, but with some good snorkelling.

FILIÁTRA BEACH
(119 F3) (*ω E9*)
Really nice, child friendly pebble beach in front of old olive trees, however at the height of summer there is often loud music and people camping rough.

GIDÁKI BEACH (119 E3) (*ω D9*)
The most beautiful, sandy pebble beach on the western shore of the bay of Vathí is only accessible on foot along a narrow track or by boat. In midsummer a small beach bar also opens.

MOTORBOATS (119 E2) (*ω D8*)
Motorboats (up to 30 h.p.) can be hired in *Kióni* harbour without a boating license.

Kioni Boat Hire | tel. 2674031144 | www.ithakagreece.com

INSIDER TIP **HIKING**

Four times per week from April to October (excluding August) Ester van Quylen offers 3–4 hour guided hikes in groups of maximum 10 people from different starting points. *15–18 euro without transfers | Island Walks | www.islandwalks.com*

ENTERTAINMENT

Theatre performances and concerts are often held in Vathí. The *Century* nightclub, on the waterfront road, is open every summer evening. The evening meeting place for the locals and Greek tourists is the café bar *Mílos*, directly on the pier.

WHERE TO STAY

CAPTAIN YIANNIS (119 F3) *(ᗠ D9)*
This spacious facility, with 11 bungalows and 12 hotel rooms, is on a gentle slope on the east side of the Bay of Vathí, it stretches down to the waterfront where there is also a swimming pool and bar. All rooms are well-appointed and individually decorated. Very good value for money! *Vathí | tel. 26 74 03 33 11 | www.captain yiannis.com | Moderate*

MÉNTOR (119 F3) *(ᗠ D9)*
Its 36 rooms and apartments make this the largest hotel on the island. Built in 1969 it is situated on the innermost end of the bay. *Vathí | tel. 26 74 03 24 33 | www.hotelmentor.gr | Moderate*

INSIDER TIP **NOSTÓS** (119 E1) *(ᗠ D8)*
Two storied, well-maintained hotel with swimming pool, 900m/2952ft from the nearest pebble beach. *27 rooms | Fríkes | tel. 26 74 03 11 00 | www.hotelnostos-ithaki.gr | Moderate–Expensive*

Chic and simple: the Perantzáda Hotel

PERANTZÁDA ... 1811 (119 F3) *(ᗠ D9)*
Boutique hotel with a villa dating from 1811 at its heart, decorated with furniture by renowned designers. *19 rooms | Vathí | tel. 26 74 02 39 14 | www.arthotel.gr | Expensive*

INFORMATION

POLYCTOR TOURS (119 F3) *(ᗠ D9)*
Platía Drakoúli | Vathí | tel. 26 74 03 31 20 | www.ithakiholidays.com
Best website about the island, very good holiday calendar: *www.ithacagreece.com*

FERRY SERVICES

Year round connections between Pisoaétos and Sámi (Kefaloniá), Fríkes and Vassilikí (Léfkas), Vathí and Pátras (Peloponnese). *Information: harbour police Vathí | tel. 26 74 03 29 09 or Delas Tours | Vathí | tel. 26 74 03 21 04*

KEFALONIÁ

The spelling of its name is just as varied as the island itself. Besides Kefaloniá, you will also see Kefallinia and Cephalonia. The diversity of Kefaloniá (pop. 36,000) is best experienced on a trip around the island. Set aside at least three days – after all the island does cover 303 square miles.

In the north, it appears as if the Érissos Peninsula seems to cling to the coast of the neighbouring island of Ithaca. There are only two villages, *Ássos* and *Fiskárdo*, on the coast and the majority of the islanders live in mountain villages in the hinterland. The lower regions of the slopes are covered in olive and cypress tress while grain, fruit and vegetables are cultivated on small plateaus. On the bare slopes of the steep west coast of the *Érissos Peninsula*, sheep and goats graze above the breathtakingly beautiful, winding scenic road.

The *Palíki Peninsula*, with *Lixoúri* as its most important town, is completely different. In the east it is bordered by the shallow, lagoon-like Bay of Argostóli and from there rises gently to the west coast which in turn falls steeply down to the Ionian Sea. Long, reddish sand beaches line the south coast with its low, white limestone cliffs, a few hotels and an almost desert-like hinterland with deep,

Photo: Napier's Lighthouse, Argostóli

Beautiful places, lots of beaches:
the largest island in the Ionian Sea
has many different aspects

dry stream valleys and mesa-like plateaus. The island's core is a powerful central mountain range with the 1131m/3710ft high, mostly barren Agía Dínami and the fir-lined 1628m/5340ft high Énos. Parallel to it, is the 1082m/3549ft high mountain range, the Kókkini Ráchi, on the east coast. In these mountainous regions there are very few settlements. That is why in the two harbour towns of Argostóli and Sámi came into being in the coastal plains with sheltered bays. Livátho, a low lying, particularly fertile region south of Argostóli, is also very densely populated.

As with everywhere else on the islands, the 1953 earthquake also caused serious damage on Kefaloniá. Towns and villages had to be rebuilt anew, only in the north, on the Érissos Peninsula, the old

The obelisk in the Bay of Argostóli commemorates the building of the causeway

character of Kefaloniá is still evident in its quiet villages.

During ancient times there were four independent town states on Kefaloniá. Ancient Pale and Pronnoi have disappeared, there are a few insignificant ruins of ancient Krane near Argostóli but at Sámi there are still large parts of the ancient city wall.

Kefaloniá is also popular with film buffs as 'Captain Corelli's Mandolin' was shot here in the summer of 2000. Directed by John Madden it stars Nicolas Cage, Penelope Cruz and John Hurt. It is set in the time of the Italian occupation of the island during the Second World War and the assassination of Italians by German soldiers in 1943.

SIGHTSEEING

ARCHAEOLOGICAL MUSEUM ●
(120 B2) (*m B12*)
On display are items from Stone Age tools through to Byzantine coins. In the last room there is a display case with objects from the Pan sanctuary of the Melissáni Cave. A clay relief shows six maidens holding hands, dancing around a horned Pan playing the flute. *Tue–Sun 8.30am–3pm | admission 3 euro s | Argostóli Odós Rókon Vergóti*

ARGOSTÓLI (120 B2) (*m B11–12*)
MAP INSIDE BACK COVER
Founded in 1757 by the Venetians, the administrative capital (pop. 9000) of the island stretches along one side of the Bay of Argostóli, without a view of the open sea. The earthquake of 1953 left only a few old buildings standing giving the town a sober and modern feel. The business life mainly takes place on the 2km/1.2mi long waterfront promenade. There you will also find the bus station and the beautiful market with its attractive, large fruit and vegetable stalls. The venue for the evening *volta*, where half of the town seems to be out on a stroll, is the *Platía Valianoú*.

In addition to the town's two museums, the main tourist attraction is the INSIDERTIP *Ágios Spiridónis* church on the main shopping street, *Odós Diad. Konstantinou*. The inside was completely painted with Byzantine frescoes during the 1970s. The lower part of the left side wall is reserved for female saints, among them the Empress Theodora, who reintroduced the veneration of icons. She is fittingly represented with an icon in her hand. The right hand side of the wall depicts only male saints. The upper part of the church represents biblical events, such as the Decent into Hell, the Healing of the Lame, the Nativity and Baptism of Christ.

The most remarkable building in the town is the causeway that was erected over the shallow bay by the British in 1813. The locals like to fish from its walls. In its centre is an obelisk, which the Kefalonians dedicated to the British in thanks for the bridge.

ÁSSOS ★
(118 C3) (*ØJ C9*)

The village of Ássos (pop. 100) lies at the inner end of a sheltered bay that is popular with yachtsmen. In the east it is bordered by terraced slopes and in the west by a headland with the remains of a 16th century *Venetian fortress (open during the day)*. It is connected to the main island by a narrow, rocky isthmus. The Venetians managed the north of the island from Ássos, the castle provided farmers protection from pirate raids. From the partially accessible ⚓ castle walls there are great views, lush greenery has grown over remnants of the building inside. During a stroll through the village, the serious damage by the 1953 earthquake is evident, Ássos never fully recovered from the quake. Only a few elderly people live here in winter, but during the summer the short pebbly beach is very popular.

AVÍTHOS LAKE (121 E2) (*ØJ D12*)

Lakes that have water all year round are a rarity in the Greek Islands so the reed thicket of the small Avíthos Lake comes a surprise. The little lake is surrounded by groves of olive trees and cypresses and is fed by several strong springs and it supplies water to the whole valley down to Póros. *On the road from Sámi to Póros, 1km before Ágios Nikólaos (signposted turnoff).*

CEPHALONIA BOTANICA ●
(120 B2) (*ØJ B12*)

On the outskirts of Argostóli a small foundation maintains a small botanical garden with a babbling brook. Information panels

---

MARCO POLO HIGHLIGHTS

★ **Ássos**
A small coastal village and a mighty fortress → p. 41

★ **Fiskárdo**
A picturesque village straight from a storybook → p. 42

★ **Monastery of Ágios Gerássimos**
A monastery that is a pilgrimage destination → p. 43

★ **Melissáni Cave**
Experience stalagmites and stalactites from a rowing boat → p. 45

★ **Ancient Sámi**
Ancient walls, Byzantine church, mountain solitude → p. 46

★ **Palíki Peninsula**
Red sandy beaches below dazzling white chalk cliffs → p. 49

list the indigenous plants in Greek and English and also give their scientific Latin names. *Tue–Sat 8.30am–3pm | free admission | on the southern outskirts of the town, signposts along the coastal road*

Míkis Theodorákis once conducted a concert here and one can only imagine what the atmosphere must have been like. *Daily 9am until dusk | admission 5 euro | on the road from Argostóli to Sámi*

ÉNOS ☀
(121 E3) *(ḍ D12)*

You can drive on a paved road up to the summit area of the highest mountain in the Ionian Islands, the 8 square mile area is a national park. When the paved road ends there is a further 7.7km/5mi long dirt track which leads via a lovely picnic spot up to the 1628m/5340ft high summit. Unfortunately the summit is marred by numerous antenna masts. In the summer months, a forester is stationed there to ensure that there are no fires in the dense forests of Kefaloniá firs. *Signposted turn-off on the Argostóli–Sámi road*

FISKÁRDO ★
(119 D1) *(ḍ C8)*

The most beautiful village on the island is on the curving shoreline of a small bay opposite Ithaca, and it was spared by the 1953 earthquake. The old, well-kept houses along the quay are the ideal backdrop for the lively hustle and bustle on the short waterfront; elegant yachts and small ferry boats enliven the port. The small village was named after the Norman ruler Robert Guiscard, who died here on one of his raids against the Byzantine Empire in 1085. The *Norman church* (its ruins seem rather incongruent in this environment) on the peninsula north of the port bay was built in his honour.

For bathing there is the shallow rocky area at the edge of the peninsula as well as two small pebble beaches on either side of the village that are only a ten minute walk away. The olive groves that line the coast offer some welcome shade.

The beach at the Bay of Fiskárdo is lined with trees that provide welcome shade

DRONGARÁTI CAVE ●
(119 D5) *(ḍ C11)*

The 44m/144ft deep stalactite cave is very effectively illuminated. The composer

KARAVÓMILOS
(119 D5) (*Ø C–D11*)

The village was newly rebuilt after 1953 and a small lake has formed between the sea and the village. The lake is a unique mixture of fresh water and sea water from sink holes in the ground below the Lássi Peninsula. There is a restored waterwheel from a former flour mill where the lake enters the Bay of Sámi. *On the road from Agía Evfímia to Sámi*

KÁSTRO ● (120 C3) (*Ø C12*)

The Livátho plain is dominated by the 320m/1050ft high mountain ridge where the island capital of Ágios Geórgios was until 1757. Today the Venetian castle, the *Kástro*, with about 600m/1970ft of walls is surrounded by a quiet little village, whose ☙ cafés and tavernas have wonderful views over the island from their terraces. *Castle May–Oct Tue–Sun 8am–7.30pm, Sun 8am–3pm | free admission | on the road from Argostóli to Skála*

INSIDER TIP MONESTARY OF ÁGIOS ANDRÉAS (120 C3) (*Ø C12*)

Opposite the Venetian castle of Ágios Geórgios lies one of the most interesting of the island monasteries. The main church houses a relic, supposedly a part of the right foot of the Apostle Andrew. More important however are the icons and frescoes in the old monastery church. The building dates back to around 1600, the oldest fresco has been dated to the 13th century. *Museum Mon–Sat 8am–2pm, monastery daily 8am–2pm and 5pm–8.30pm | admission 3 euros | south of the road from Argostóli to Skála*

MONASTERY OF ÁGIOS GERÁSSIMOS
★ ● (121 D2) (*Ø C12*)

The most visited monastery on the island stands on the edge of the Ómalon plain 400m/1312ft above the sea level surrounded by mountains. In this region, the famous INSIDER TIP Robóla wine is cultivated and pressed in the ● cellars of the wine cooperative near the monastery. *(Visit to the Robóla Cooperative Winery incl. wine tasting April–Oct daily 9am–9pm, Nov–March Mon–Fri 7am–9pm | free tastings | www.robola.gr).*

The first impression of the imposing, marble-clad new church monastery is the kilometre-long, straight avenue that leads up to it. The old monastery church is more pleasant and modest, and in front of it are some of the plane trees that were planted by the saint himself in the 16th century. One of the frescoes in the interior shows the deathbed of St Gerássimos, whose soul is represented as a swaddled

SEA WATERMILLS

Usually water flows from the land into the sea. At Argostóli, where the coast lifted almost 50cm during the earthquake of 1953, things are a little different. Here the Ionian Sea flows into underground channels on the Lássi Peninsula, travels under the island and then re-emerges as fresh water kilometres away in the Melissáni Cave and at Karavómilos. At Argostóli where the sea flowed inland, the power of the sea water was harnessed by a large watermill built in the 19th century. The mill has been restored and now forms part of a taverna, it is open to the public.

infant already committed to Christ. The bones of the saint rest in a coffin and can by kissed by pilgrims through two small openings. At certain times, a priest reads prayers that believers have written on small pieces of paper. A trapdoor in the church floor, leads down a steep ladder down into a cave where the island's saint once lived. *April–Oct daily 3.30am–1pm and 3.30pm–8pm, otherwise 4am–1pm and 3pm–7pm | entrance signposted along the Argostóli–Sámi road*

MONASTERY OF KIPURÉON
(118 A6) (*ω A11*)
A few monks still live here, 100m/328ft above the remote and inaccessible west coast of the Palíki Peninsula. The monastery church houses beautiful icons, among them one showing the three most important island saints of the Ionian Islands.

KORGIALÉNIOS LIBRARY
(120 B2) (*ω B12*)
The library is the foundation of a rich Kefalonian who died in 1920; the building was faithfully restored after the 1953 earthquake. On display in the basement are various icons, folk art objects, costumes, furniture, agricultural and domestic appliances as well as historical photos. *Mon–Sat 9am–2pm | admission 4 euros | Argostóli Odós Ilía Zérvon*

KOURKOUMELÁTA
(120 C3) (*ω C12*)
The quiet village is probably the most beautiful and well-kept in the entire district of Liváthos, which was particularly hard hit by the 1953 earthquake. The majority of the inhabitants back then were sailors. A shipping family supported them after the catastrophe with generous donations, many attractive houses were built. Today the gardens and streets are carefully maintained, making for a pleasant short stroll through the village which you can follow with a visit to the central village café of *Marína (Budget)*.

LÁSSI PENINSULA
(120 B2) (*ω B11–12*)
The hilly peninsula, where the island's capital Argostóli is situated, can also be explored on foot. On the way from Argostóli to the headland you will see the restored *waterwheels* of two sea water mills. The first one is situated on the premises of the Thalassómilos restaurant, and the second is at the burnt-out restaurant O Mílos Katovóthres.
The British built a small *round temple* in the Doric style on the headland, which served as a beacon at the harbour entrance. After the 1953 earthquake, it was rebuilt in a simplified manner. A little further a signposted road branches off the coastal road and leads 700m to the

Enchanted light: boat trip on the crystal clear waters of the shimmering lake in the Melissáni Cave

Monumento Caduti. The memorial commemorates the 9470 Italian soldiers, who after the Italy's capitulation in September 1942 refused to surrender to German troops and were consequently killed.

LIXOÚRI
(120 B1–2) (*□ B11*)

The capital (pop. 3500) of the Palíki Peninsula was founded in 1534 and still exudes the kind of grace and gentility which most towns on the Ionian Islands lost after the 1953 earthquake. The market centre spreads out around the bus station and the social centre is the large *platía.* One of the villas in the upper part of the town, today serves as a ● *museum and library (Tue–Fri 9am–1.30pm, Sat 9.30am–12.30pm | free admission).* Some of the rooms have partially restored ceilings that were painted over 100 years ago, furniture from every period as well as some icons are also on display. *Frequent*

ferry service between Argostóli and Lixoúri around the clock

MELISSÁNI CAVE ★
(119 D5) (*□ C10*)

A visit to the stalactite cave is a unique experience as a good part of it is a small lake accessible by boat. The sun filters through an opening which is framed by green trees and the light makes the crystal clear water shimmer in hues of blue and green. In the back of the cave, the water laps a small islet which was once the site of a Pan sanctuary. Archaeological findings from the sanctuary are now exhibited in the Archaeological Museum of Argostóli. *Daily 9am–sundown | admission 7 euros*

METAXÁTA (120 C3) (*□ C12*)

Like most of the villages in the Livátho plain, Metaxáta was almost entirely rebuilt after the 1953 earthquake. It has some very attractive villas and gardens. Near the village numerous shaft and chamber tombs from the late Mycenaean era were uncovered and there are some excavations here and there. *Access: turn off from the road between Peratáta and Metaxáta just behind the signposted turnoff to the monastery of Ágios Andréas onto an unmarked dirt track and after 250m you will reach the fenced excavations.*

PÓROS

(121 F2) (*M E12*)

The small harbour village (pop. 900) slowly evolved into a tourism centre but it is still very serene and calm. About 500m above the village and 6km/3.7mi on foot is the oldest monastery on the island, *Moní tis Panagías tis Atroú*. The first written evidence of it dates back to 1264. Behind the modern building, where the monks now live, the ☀ old monastery and chapels rise up in the magnificent mountain solitude with superb views of the coast and the Peloponnese. *Access: just short of a mile from the shore the road branches off to a ravine on the Póros–Argostóli road*

SÁMI

(119 E5) (*M D11*)

Sámi (pop. 1100) stretches out at the foot of a mountain, where the ancient city walls are still plainly visible. In the town itself there is a *Roman chamber tomb* and the 5m/16ft high brick walls of a preserved *Roman bath*.

To reach the ruins of ★ *Ancient Sámi* follow the signposted road at the north-eastern edge of the village to the *Monastery of Agrílion* (rebuilt after the 1953 earthquake) where the road forks for the second time, and a sign to the left leads to the monastery, you take the road to the right. The ancient city wall that runs along the hill is clearly visible. At the point named *Kástro*

In the south-east there are beautiful beaches such as the sandy beach at Skála

you reach a white chapel almost at the dirt road. Right next to it is the ruin of a medieval monastery church and an ancient watchtower. Its preserved walls of carefully hewn stone reach up to 5m/16ft. A few minutes' walk from here, in the woods below the white chapel, are the ruins of a medieval church *Ágios Nikólaos (open to the public)*. A long, narrow sandy beach stretches from Sámi almost to Karavómilos.

SKÁLA
(121 F4) *(🗺 E13)*

At the southern end of the small seaside resort (pop. 550) are the well preserved foundations of a *Roman villa (daily 8.30am–3pm | free admission)*. A protective roof shelters two well preserved floor mosaics. One depicts the sacrifice of three animals, and the other one a young man who symbolises envy.

Towards Póros are numerous sand and pebble beaches without tourist facilities. Between the slopes and the sea is the white *Ágios Geórgios chapel* as well as the small remains of an ancient 6th century BC temple.

TZANÁTA
(121 F3) *(🗺 E12)*

In the village centre, a brown signpost leads the way to a Mycenaean *Thólos tomb* dating back to the time around 1350 BC. The burial chamber under the grave mound is open to the public. *(Tue–Sun 8.30am–3pm | free admission | 400m right of the main road to Póros).*

FOOD & DRINK

INSIDER TIP ▶ BELL TOWER CAFÉ ●
(120 B2) *(🗺 B12)*

The café in the bell tower on the promenade is run by a local disability organisation and serves traditional sweets and refreshing drinks such as almond milk *soumáda* and plum *vissináda*. The interior is decorated with historical photos and you can climb the 75 up the tower. *Daily from 8am | Argostóli | Odós Lithostrótou 52B | Budget*

CASA GREC **(120 B2)** *(🗺 B12)*

Well-kept restaurant run by a Canadian couple who speak English and French. They serve modern Mediterranean cuisine, excellent steaks and good wine. *Daily from 7.30pm | Argostóli | Odós St. Metaxá 10 | Expensive*

INSIDER TIP ▶ KÁSTRO
(120 C3) *(🗺 C12)*

The taverna at the entrance to the Venetian castle is a shady idyll in a sea of flowers. The host Spíros and his wife Níki serve affordable lunches, delicious cakes and inexpensive cocktails, always accompanied by Greek music. *May–Oct daily from 9am | Kástro | Budget*

MOLFETAS ⏱
(120 C2) (*∅ B11*)

The restaurant and guesthouse (6 rooms) in a restored old house in at Argostóli are both stylishly decorated with antiques. The hostess prepares tea from herbs that she collects herself and she makes an excellent chocolate mousse; the meat served is also organic. *Farakláta | tel. 26 71 08 40 07 | www.georgemolfetas.com | Expensive*

INSIDER TIP O AGRAPÍDOS ⌖ ⏱
(120 F2) (*∅ E12*)

Very inexpensive taverna serving hearty Greek food, with a magnificent view. Wine from their own vineyard, homemade bread, vegetables from their own garden. *Póros | above the harbour on the road to Skála | Budget*

PAPARAZZI (120 B2) (*∅ B12*)

A restaurant run by young Italians. Lots of pizza and pasta. Reservations recommended. *Daily from 7.30pm | Argostóli | Odós Lavráka 2 | tel. 26 71 02 26 31 | Moderate*

TASSÍA (119 D1) (*∅ C8*)

Renowned restaurant on the quay, known for their fresh lobster and crayfish. Six fishermen work exclusively for this restaurant that also serves meat dishes. The proprietor Tassía Dendrinoú has also written a Kefalonian cookbook that is available in English at the restaurant. *Fiskárdo | Expensive*

VASSO'S (119 D1) (*∅ C8*)

Taverna on the promenade of the yacht marina and fishing harbour. Good selection of warm dishes. During the early summer swallows nest in the guest room. *Fiskárdo | Expensive*

SHOPPING

ROBÓLA
(120 B2) (*∅ B12*)

The small shop, named after the famous grape, stocks all the wines from the local cooperative at affordable prices. Decent wines are also sold on tap. *Argostóli | at the market*

VOSKOPOÚLA
(120 B2) (*∅ B12*)

This confectionary has produced typical Kefalonian sweets since 1910. Especially worth trying is the paste made of dried quinces. *Argostóli | Odós Lithostráto 3 (next to the court) | www.voskopoula.gr*

SPORTS & ACTIVITIES

ANTÍSAMOS
(119 E5) (*∅ D10*)

5km/3mi northeast of Sámi this half mile long pebble beach is best known for being the set of numerous scenes from 'Captain Corelli's Mandolin'. Its turquoise water is surrounded by trees.

KAMÍNIA BEACH
(121 F4) (*∅ E13*)

Miles of isolated, shallow beach in the extreme south of the island opposite Zákynthos. *Access signposted on the Skála–Ratzaklí road*

MAKRÍS GIÁLOS & PLATÍS GIÁLOS
(120 B2) (*∅ B12*)

Beautiful sandy beach with a taverna, lots of water sport activities and sun lounger rentals. Very popular in summer. On Argostóli side of the Lássi Peninsula. *Hourly bus connections to nearby Argostóli*

The isolated Monastery of Kipoúrion is enthroned high above the sea on the Palíki Peninsula

NATURAL HEALTH RETREAT ●
(120 C3) (*M B12*)

Chris and Joan Philips from Bournemouth offer first class Reiki treatments, Swedish body massages, Indian head and shoulder massages and reflexology treatments. They are open all year round. *Svoronáta | tel. 26 71 04 23 26 | www.kefalonianhr. co.uk | massage 37 euros/1 hour*

PALÍKI PENINSULA ★
(120 A–B2) (*M A–B12*)

There are many quiet, isolated beaches on the Palíki Peninsula. Red sand stretches from the low, white cliff coast along the entire southern coast of the peninsula from Lepéde to Kounópetra. The clay from the high cliffs is traditionally used by the Greeks for cosmetic facial masks. The almost 20m wide *Xi Beach,* with its shallow sloping shore line, is particularly beautiful, as is the wide crescent shaped *Vatsá Beach* with a small fishing harbour at a river mouth.

ENTERTAINMENT

BASS CLUB (120 B2) (*M B12*)

The island's trendy dance club; every Thursday at around 11pm it is modern 'Greek Night' (guaranteed no folk music), Fri and Sat international dance music until at least 3.30am. *Argostóli | Odós R. Vergóti | www.bassclub.gr*

BODEGA (120 B2) (*M B12*)

Pub that has a wide variety of different beers and small snacks, some evenings also live music. Young and old meet here. *Daily from 10am | Argostóli | Odós Rizospáston*

INSIDER TIP ► PUB OLD HOUSE ●
(120 B2) (*M B12*)

Listen to rock music, from Pink Floyd to current music, at the long bar counter, also a small garden and Leftéris, the friendly host. *Daily from 8.30pm | Argostóli | Odos Rizospáston/Odós Harboúri 13–15*

AÉNOS
(120 B2) (*ff B12*)

Decorated with antiques, this stylish hotel is the best in Argostólis. *33 rooms | Platía Valianoú | tel. 26 71 02 80 13 | www.aenos. com | Expensive*

INSIDER TIP ANEMÓMILOS ☺ ⋙
(118 C3) (*ff C9*)

The small guesthouse run by the organic farmer Gerássimos is on a low hill surrounded by a bizarre mesa landscape. In the *Kafenío Panórama* just next door his daughter Dimítra serves regional delicacies that you will seldom find anywhere else. *5 rooms | Mantzavináta | tel. 26 71 09 17 55 | petdimi@yahoo.gr | Budget*

INSIDER TIP DREAMS
(121 F4) (*ff E13*)

A large lawn separates the eight studios from the beach and the beach bar, where you can also have breakfast. The proprietor Panayíis is also very proud of his cocktail recipes. The studios can accommodate up to four people and the owner speaks excellent English. Very good value for money, open all year round. *Katélios | Ágios Barbara Beach | tel. 26 74 09 26 94 | www. agnitravel.com | Budget*

GERÁNIA
(118 C3) (*ff C9*)

A peaceful guesthouse situated in a large garden, 300m from the shore. Parking available. *12 rooms | Ássos | tel. 26 74 05 15 26 | www.pensiongerania.gr | Moderate*

IONIAN PLAZA
(120 B2) (*ff B12*)

The best town hotel on the island offers superb value for money. *47 rooms | Argostóli | Platía Vallianoú | tel. 26 71 02 55 81 | www.ionianplaza.gr | Expensive*

KARAVÁDOS BEACH
(121 D3) (*ff B12*)

Hotel with swimming pool in the countryside some 150m from the beach and 2km/1.2mi east of Karavádos. Old fashioned, but comfortably furnished rooms in five individual buildings. *77 rooms | Karavádos | tel. 26 71 06 94 00 | www. kbhotel.gr | Moderate*

LINÁRDOS ⋙
(118 C3) (*ff C9*)

Three-storey guesthouse only metres from the sea, all the simply and tastefully decorated rooms offer stunning views of the Bay of Ássos and the peninsula with its castle. Great value for money. *11 rooms | Ássos | tel. 26 74 05 15 63 | www.linardos apartments.gr | Budget*

RÉGINA RENT ROOMS ⋙
(119 D1) (*ff C8*)

Guesthouse on the main car park 50m above the harbour, ten rooms all with sea views, five more rooms in the town. *Fiskárdo | tel. 26 74 04 11 25 | Budget– Moderate*

INSIDER TIP TRÍFILLI
(121 D3) (*ff D12*)

Three Greek brothers and a Swiss lady run this friendly and engaging guesthouse that is overgrown with flowers, it also has an excellent taverna. Just a few hundred metres from the beach. *Lourdáta | tel. 26 71 03 11 14 | www.trifilli.com | Budget*

INSIDER TIP VATSA CLUB ●
(120 A2) (*ff A12*)

A hidden paradise right at the very end of the peninsula, the club overlooks the sea at a river mouth. There is a quaint beach taverna and four two-storey chalets with modern furnished double rooms and kitchens. You will not need anything other than your swimsuit here. *Ágios*

Nikólaos | tel. 69 77 63 10 53 | www.vatsa. gr | Expensive

WHITE ROCKS
(120 B3) (*M̶ B12)

The hotel complex and garden bungalows are spread over 14 acres of old pine forest right on the sea. The beach is only access-

FERRY CONNECTIONS

All year round, daily from Sámi to Pátras (Peloponnese), Pisoaétos and Vathí (Ithaca) also from Fiskárdo to Vassilikí (Léfkas).

All year round between Agía Evfimía and Vathí (Ithaca) as well as Ástakos (main-

Let the holiday begin! Travel to Kefaloniá on the eponymous ferry

able from the water and from the hotel grounds. The entire facility was modernised in 2012 and was upgraded to be environmentally and energy-friendly. *163 rooms | Platís Giálos | tel. 26 71 02 31 67 | www.whiterocks.gr | Expensive*

INFORMATION

TOURISM BOARD
(120 B2) (*M̶ B12)
Argostóli | coast road, near the ferry harbour | tel. 26 71 02 22 48

land) and between Argostóli, Póros and Killíni (Peloponnese).

From May to October twice daily between Pessáda in the south of the island and Skinári (Zákynthos).

In midsummer daily, otherwise twice weekly between Fiskárdo and Fríkes (Ithaca) as well as Nidrí (Léfkas).

In the summer several times a day between Argostóli and Kellíni (Peloponnese) also between Sámi and Igoumenítsa (mainland), Páxi and Corfu. *Information: harbour police in Argostóli | tel. 26 71 02 22 24*

LÉFKAS

Léfkas, often called Lefkáda in Greece, is the only one of the Ionian Island that is connected to the mainland by a bridge. And it is proof of the Greek art of improvisation: instead of building an expensive new one, they converted a matching sized ferry and berthed it sideways in the 50m/164ft wide canal that has made Léfkas (pop. 24,000) an island since Roman times. If a ship needs to pass, the 'bridge' simply swings aside.

Just behind the original bridge at the north-eastern tip of the island, the road splits in two. One leads over a dam that was built by the British, to the capital *Lefkáda*. The other circles around the lagoon in the north and also passes along a half mile sandy beach with dunes and the ideal conditions for windsurfers.

The coastal villages are almost exclusively on the eastern side of the island. In almost every one of them one has the impression that one is standing on the shore of a lake that is surrounded by mountains and hills. In the north only a narrow sound separates Léfkas from the Acarnanian mainland, further to the south peninsulas and small islands on the horizon create borders.

One of these islands is *Skórpios*, the private island of the Onassis family. The only noteworthy village on the rest of the coast

Photo: Cape Doukáto

Interplay of sea and land: from the dunes in the north to the chalk cliffs in the south – a paradise for beach lovers

is the beautiful *Vassilikí* in a wide bay in the south-west.

Towards the Ionian Sea the bay is bordered by the *Lefkáta Peninsula* with a coastline of high white chalk cliffs that drop off into the sea. The coastline is dotted with idyllic sandy coves such as *Pórto Katsíki* while at other spots there are miles of isolated beaches that difficult to reach. Those seeking peace and quiet on the

island (35km/21mi long and 15km/9mi wide) will find it in the mountain villages high above the west coast and in the interior of the island. Here there are also some lovely hikes. Léfkas does not have a lot to offer those looking for educational trips, little remains of the ancient town of Corinth that was founded here in 640 BC and there is also hardly anything from the Venetian era, due to the 24 earthquakes

Neo-classical church building in Lefkáda from the Venetian era

that have ravaged the island since the 15th century. However, those who are in search of some beautiful beaches will feel right at home on the island.

SIGHTSEEING

ÁGIOS NIKÍTAS (116 B2) (𝄞 C4)
The only seaside resort (pop. 110) is on the west coast, it is nestled in a valley so narrow that there is only enough space for a (pedestrian) street. The beach in front of the resort, is only about 50m; a longer sandy beach stretches to the north. It is especially popular with tourists with camper vans.

INSIDER TIP ARCHAEOLOGICAL MUSEUM (116 C1) (𝄞 D3)
Modern museum in the cultural centre of Léfkas, where temporary exhibitions are also held. The museum exhibits finds from the archaeological excavations on the island and many of the exhibits are well explained.

The first cabinet, right next to the cashier, showcases ancient music. Four movable terracotta dolls from the graves the 5th century BC children are on show in Hall C. There are also stone urns and tomb monuments and a small part of the ancient cemetery has been reconstructed. Hall D is dedicated to the German archaeologist Wilhelm Dörpfeld and his findings. *Tue–Sun 8.30am–3pm | admission 2 euros | Lefkáda | Odós Ang. Sikelianoú/Odós N. Svorónou (at the northern end of the coast road)*

KALAMÍTSI (116 C3) (𝄞 C4)
The small inland village (pop. 200) above the long sandy beach of *Káthisma* lies 380m/1246ft above the west coast. On the one hand it is very rural: chickens,

goats and donkeys walk freely through the gardens and fields, the whole village seems rustic and messy. On the other hand there are also a number of guest-houses and private rooms, a few tavernas and even a modern café club where, unfortunately, they play music loudly, even during the day.

KARIÁ (116 B2–3) (*◫ D4*)

The largest mountain village (pop. 1000) on the island still has many traditional houses. The village square is shaded by old plane trees and has a good taverna, and is full of life in the afternoon. At the top end of the village there is also a small, private *ethnological museum (daily 9am–9pm).*

MONASTERY OF FANEROMÉNIS (116 C1) (*◫ D3*)

The only monastery on the island that is still inhabited lies in a small grove above the lagoon and the town. It has recently been extensively restored and now also includes a beautiful garden. A monastery museum is currently under construction. The evening services that take place every Wednesday between 8pm and midnight are particularly atmospheric. *Closed 2pm–4pm | 4km/2.4mi above Lefkáda on the road to Ágios Nikítas*

LEFKÁDA (116 C1) (*◫ D3*)

MAP INSIDE BACK COVER

The special charm of the island's capital (pop. 7000) lies in its position – between the lagoon and narrow strait that separates Léfkas from the mainland. The alleys of the town are lined with houses that survived the 1953 earthquake because their upper storeys were built in the Turkish tradition with wood rather than stone. These wooden facades are unfortunately often clad in sheets of metal or synthetic materials giving the island's capital a rather distinctive and temporary feel.

However, many of its streets and alleys are paved and attractive, and many facades are painted in various pastel shades giving it an authentic Mediterranean look. A few churches from the Venetian era have been preserved although they are marred by some truly ugly bell towers that were replaced after the 1953 quake.

The social centre of the town is the *platía* with its kiosks and cafés. Here, just next to the Ágios Spirídonis church, is the start of *Odós Dimarhou Verrioti* with its authentic handcraft workshops – from coffin makers to icon painters and even dental technicians – and you can watch them at work through the window. The main shopping streets are the largely pedestrian *Odós Derpfeld* and its extension that ends at the street market *Odós Méla*, commonly referred to as *agorá*. The many café bars along the fishing harbour embankment are busy in the evening.

LEFKÁTA PENINSULA
(116 A5–6) (*ω C6–7*)

The white chalk cliffs of the Lefkáta Peninsula offer some of the most beautiful coastal scenery in Greece. The road is paved up to the Bay of Pórto Katsíki; thereafter a good dirt road leads south to

The waterfall at Nídri only flows from autumn to spring

★ *Cape Doukáto* where a solitary lighthouse overlooks the ships that constantly pass by on the route between Italy and the Gulf of Pátras. In antiquity this was also the site of a Temple of Apollo. Every year on the Apollo feast day a condemned man was thrown from the cape strapped with bird wings – those who survived were freed.

Between Athaní and the Cape Doukáto another road branches off to the ★ *Bay of Pórto Katsíki* a pale strip of beach beneath a white chalk cliff. This lovely beach often appears on posters promoting Greek tourism. From Athaní there are roads and tracks leading to several other excellent beaches.

LIGIÁ (116 C2) (*ω D4*)

The unassuming little village with its small pebble beach is one of the largest fishing centres of western Greece. Numerous large *kaíkis* (traditional wooden boats) anchor in the harbour and the coffee shops along the quayside are all geared towards the fishermen.

NIDRÍ (116 C3) (*ω D5*)

The liveliest holiday resort on the island (and also its main ferry terminal) is scenically situated opposite the entrance to the green fringed Bay of Vlichó. Its bustling centre is the harbour, where ferries depart for Meganísi, Ithaca and Kefaloniá. This is also where you can find excursion boats to the Onassis island of Skórpios and for trips around the island and cruises to other Ionian Islands. There is a **INSIDER TIP** *monument* to Aristotle Onassis (1906–75) the famous Greek shipping magnate, billionaire and husband of Jacqueline Kennedy.

Take a beautiful hike from here to the *waterfall* that is situated 3km/1.8mi from here in a small, narrow gorge, which only has water until May. On the southern edge of the village the main road cuts through an early Bronze Age *necropolis* with 33 tombs which was excavated from 1905–12. However, there are only a few tombs (signposted with 'Early Bronze Age Tumuli') that are identifiable. Opposite Nidrí lies the small island of Madoúri and the neo-classical villa belonging to the Lefkadian poet, Aristotle Valaorítis (1824–79).

SANTA MAURA
(116 C1) (*Ⓜ D–E3*)

During the Middle Ages the island's capital was around the walls of this for-tress on the mainland side of the canal that separates Léfkas from Acarnania. In its current form it dates back to the year 1684.

SIVÓTA (116 C5) (*Ⓜ D6*)

The former fishing village on a narrow, sheltered bay is especially charming at night, when dozens of yachts anchor here. On the fjord-like bay there are only tiny pebble beaches but there are numerous fish tavernas and bars right on the shore all lying in wait for the wealthy evening public.

INSIDER TIP VASSILIKÍ
(116 B5) (*Ⓜ C6*)

There are still a few old houses in this vil-lage (pop. 370) on the inside of a wide bay that is ideal for windsurfers. The waterfront is lined by countless restaurants shaded by tall eucalyptus trees and a long pebble beach starts right at the edge of the village. Excursion boats depart from the village quay to the sandy beaches of the Lefkáta Peninsula, and car ferries to Ithaca and Kefaloniá.

VLICHÓ
(116 C4) (*Ⓜ D5*)

Vlichó lies on the inner end of the bay and is surrounded by green hills. On the outskirts of the village there is a small, traditional shipyard where *kaíkis* is still built and repaired. From Vlichó a narrow road leads to the wooded peninsula of

Xerónisso with numerous small and beau-tiful beaches.

CIAO (116 C1) (*Ⓜ D3*)

Although the selection at this small ice cream parlour is limited, all the ice cream is homemade from fresh milk and cream. *Lefkáda | Odós Mitropóleos 8*

FRÍNI (116 C1) (*Ⓜ D3*)

Hostess Fríni is known for her fast service and snappy banter and she is also very creative in the kitchen, with dishes such as fig salad with grilled goat's cheese. *Lefkáda | Odós Golémos 12 (on the coast road opposite the pier) | Moderate*

LIGHTHOUSE (116 C1) (*Ⓜ D3*)

A small, well-established taverna with a sheltered garden where you can sit

LOW BUDGET

▶ To see where Onassis and family spent their money, you need not book a boat trip around Skórpios. You can also see the island up close, but without a swim, if you take the Meganísi ferry which passes very close to Skórpios. The return trip will only coast approx. 4 euros and you can even visit Meganísi.

▶ The *Kafenío Karfákis* is inexpensive and good. A Greek coffee only costs 1.30 euros while 0.2l glass of red wine and a small fish with chips, olives, peppers, beans, tomatoes and bread costs a mere 2.50 euros! *Daily from 8am | Lefkáda | Odós Stratigoú Méla 127*

quietly and enjoy delicious Greek specialities. Host Sotíris spent some time in Washington D.C. and speaks excellent English. Reservations are recommended. *Daily from 5pm | Lefkáda | Odós Filarmonikís 14 | tel. 26 45 02 51 17 | Moderate*

NAUTILUS (116 C1) (*🗺 D3*)

The rustic wooden furniture in the restaurant was made by the owner himself. Even the pizza dough is homemade; the suppliers of the meat, sausage and cheese are indicated on the menu. The toppings are generous, the prices are very fair. *Lefkáda | Kentrikí Platía | Budget*

INSIDER TIP OÁSIS ☺

(116 A5) (*🗺 C6*)

Forest taverna with tables under the trees. Lamb and goat from their own butchery, wild rabbits, sheep's milk yogurt and homemade cheese. *On the road, 8km/5mi from Athaní to Pórto Katsíiki | Moderate*

O GIÁNNIS (116 C2) (*🗺 D4*)

Rustic fish taverna, some of the tables and chairs are right on the narrow pebble beach. *Ligiá | in the harbour | Expensive*

O MÍNAS (116 C3) (*🗺 D4*)

This taverna is more than 40 years old and was named after the host's grandfather. It is regarded by many Lefkadians as the best fish taverna on the island, particularly as the family also have their own fishing boat. *Nikianá | on the main road | Moderate*

INSIDER TIP O PLÁTANOS

(116 C3) (*🗺 D5*)

Garden taverna owned by an Athenian dentist and amateur chef. Lamb and pork chops are sold according to weight, specialities are roast lamb and lamb liver. *Daily from 8.30pm | Vafkéri | at the church on the main road | Moderate*

PANORAMIC VIEW ☼

(116 A4) (*🗺 C5*)

Taverna with a fabulous view where all the dishes are prepared by the host family. Wide selection of vegetarian specialities, excellent spaghetti. *Athaní | on the town square | Budget*

PIPÉRI (116 C3) (*🗺 D5*)

The chic and stylish restaurant in Nidrí harbour offers unusual specialities from all over Greece, such as the mixed salad *politikí* from Macedonia, the split pea dip *fáva* from Santorini and lamb in a yogurt sauce, a dish from the area now known as Turkish Smýrna (Izmir). There are also several Greek cheeses available. *Nidrí | on the harbourside, 20m south of the ferry terminal to Meganísi | Expensive*

PLÓTO

(116 C1) (*🗺 D3*)

This meeting spot for the island's youth (day and night) is a bar housed on the two decks a replica sailing ship. During the day, Távli and Monopoly are played, at night hip music. *Lefkáda*

RACHÍ ☼ ☺

(116 B2) (*🗺 C4*)

This venue impresses with its terrace with fantastic views of the sea and the coastal hamlet of Kalamítsi. Wine and oil comes from their own harvest, the many legumes on offer are cultivated in the immediate vicinity. In midsummer you will need to make a reservation. *Exanthia | at the entrance to the village, behind the bakery | tel. 26 45 09 94 39 | Budget*

INSIDER TIP SÉSOULAS ☺

(116 A4) (*🗺 C5*)

Hostess Georgiá serves her guests vegetables and salads from her own garden, even the chickens are from her coop and the meat is also local. With simple peas-

Blue and white: the sea at Ágios Nikítas looks like it could have been the template for the Greek flag

ant dishes, such as *pastítsio* or stuffed tomatoes and peppers, Sélousas is so authentic that if feels like the Greece of yesteryear. *Drágano | along the main road | Budget*

YACHT BAR (116 C5) (*ⱷ D6*)

The bar at the south-western end of Sivóta's waterfront is the most beautiful place to enjoy an afternoon drink and watch yachtsmen arrive. Also popular as a late nightcap venue. *Daily from 8am.*

SHOPPING

INSIDER TIP PANAJÓTIS FRANGOÚLIS (116 C1) (*ⱷ D3*)

The shop is also a distillery and the oúzo, brandy and various liqueurs that you can buy here are also produced on site. *Lefkáda | Odós Mitropóleos 4 | www. fragoulis.com*

STAVRÁKAS (116 C1) (*ⱷ D3*)

The Stavrákas family has been making Lefkadian sweets for more than 55 years. You absolutely have to try the fig salami made with dried figs, honey, nuts, sesame and spices as well as the sugar-free chocolate with prunes. *Lefkáda | Odós Derpfeld 22 | www.stavrakas-shop.com*

STAVROÚLA STAVRÁKA (116 B3) (*ⱷ D4*)

The linen and cotton embroidery sold in this shop are all made by the women of the village. *Kariá | at the upper end of the Platía*

SPORTS & BEACHES

Léfkas is a Mecca for active holidaymakers, especially popular with wind and kite surfers are Lefkáda and Vassilikí *(see p. 93)*.

Brigitte Roth offers guided herb hikes where you can learn how to recognise and collect medicinal plants. Brigitte has been living in Greece since 1986 and as a qualified phytotherapist she really knows her plants *(approx. 6 hour hike 25 euros, 2 day seminar 80 euro | tel. 26 45 04 13 09 | www.lefkas.cc)*.

Get Active in Nidrí offer a wide variety of guided mountain bike rides to suit all abilities and budgets *(www.getactive lefkas.com/Welcome.html)*.

The most beautiful beaches are situated on the spit of Lefkáda north of the lagoon, on the Bay of Vassilikí and below Athaní on the Lefkáta Peninsula (Pórto Katsíki, Giálos und Egrémni Beach).

Very popular beaches include Ágios Nikítas and Káthisma on the north-west coast and the beach 5km/3mi below the village of Póros on the south coast. Less frequented is the pebble beach of Mílos which one can reach on foot from Ágios Nikítas (25 minutes).

ENTERTAINMENT

Dance club lovers will be disappointed on Léfkas as the club selection is very limited. The liveliest (also during the day) is the outdoor disco café, the *Sail-Inn* (Nidrí | on the beach towards Lefkáda) and in the dance club *Tropicana* (Nidrí | at the southern end of the main thorough-fare). In the island's capital the youth meet up in *Kárma* (Lefkáda | Odós Derpfeld 1).

Two great music cafés right on the beach, where the sound of waves mixes with the sounds of CDs are the café club *Liotrívi* (Sivóta) and the **INSIDER TIP** *Kafetéria On The Rock* (Ágios Nikítas). Sailors, artists, tourists and intellectuals alike all meet in the *Havana Cuba Bar* (Lefkáda | Odós Spírou Gházi) where the music is softer and Mojitos are the drinks of choice.

WHERE TO STAY

CASA CAMPOS (116 C1) (*M D3*)

Three double-storey studios for 2–4 persons in four houses painted in colourful Ionian colours. The maisonettes are set in over an acre garden with old olive trees and a large swimming pool. Modern and very tastefully furnished, 10–15 minutes to the town centre and to the beaches, open all year round. *Lefkáda | south-west of the town | mobile tel. 69 83 76 46 05 | www.casacampos.gr | Moderate–Expensive*

FANTÁSTICO ☼ (116 B2) (*M C4*)

Studios and apartments for 2–5 persons on a fantastic hillside location with sea views. *8 apartments | Kalamítsi | on the town outskirts | tel. 26 45 09 93 90 | Budget*

LÉFKAS (116 C1) (*M D3*)

Largest hotel in the island's capital, at the start of the causeway to the mainland. Three-storey, modern finishes, most of the rooms have sea views. *93 rooms | Lefkáda | Odós Panagoú 2 | tel. 26 45 02 39 16 | www.hotel-lefkas.gr | Moderate*

ODÉON ☼ (116 B5) (*M C6*)

Modern studios and apartments with balconies and beautiful views, in a house with a swimming pool, right on the beach and 800m from the town centre. *17 apartments | Vassilikí | off the road towards Komílio | tel. 26 45 03 19 18 | www.vassiliki. com | Moderate–Expensive*

INSIDER TIP ▶ PIROFÁNI (116 C1) (*M D3*)

Modern guesthouse, centrally located, good value for money, friendly host family. All rooms with balconies, air conditioning and fridges. *18 rooms | Lefkáda | Odós Derpfeld 36 | tel. 26 45 02 58 44 | lefkastown-hotelpirofani.clickhere.gr | Moderate*

PORTO GALINI (116 C3) *(ⅅ D5)*

This hotel is harmoniously integrated into the surrounding landscape. It has 136 large rooms in 39 single and double-storey buildings set above a small pebble beach in a quiet area. The establishment has received an award for good hotel architecture. Wide range of watersport facilities, generous ☆ spa with indoor pool overlooking the sea. *Maganá Nikianás | 4km/ 2.4mi north of Nidrí below the coastal road | tel. 26 45 09 24 31 | www.portogalini.gr | Expensive*

PORTO KATSIKI STUDIOS ☆
(116 A4) *(ⅅ C5)*

The complex lies in a beautiful, scenic location and offers rooms and studios for up to four persons, good parking options and a small garden. Excellent value for money! *8 rooms | Athaní | at the lower end of town | tel. 26 45 03 31 36 | www.porto katsikistudios.com | Budget*

INSIDERTIP ▶ ROUDA BAY
(116 C5) *(ⅅ D6)*

The complex features buildings with natural stone, tiled roofs and many also with typical Lefkadian wooden facades. It is set in a truly paradisiacal garden and each suite different, and all are furnished to a high standard. The maisonettes offer accommodation for up to 6 persons. *28 rooms | Póros | on the coast road | tel. 26 45 09 56 34 | Moderate*

SOFIAS STUDIOS ☆
(116 C5) *(ⅅ D6)*

The six simply decorated studios, owned by the friendly and helpful hostess Sofía,

BOOKS & FILMS

▶ **The Odyssey** – The 2700 year old Homeric epic is available in several English editions, in both verse and prose form. It is also available in a series of audio CDs. 'The Odyssey' has also been made into a film many times, such as by Mario Camerini with Kirk Douglas and Silvana Mangano (1954, 2 DVDs) and as a TV series with Armand Assante and Greta Scacchi (1997, DVD)

▶ **It's All Greek to Me!: A Tale of a Mad Dog and an Englishman, Ruins, Retsina – And Real Greeks** – This memoir by John Mole (2006) is a witty and entertaining glimpse into life in a picturesque Greek village. The humorous story follows his family's decision to purchase a ruined house and the characters who help them to fix it up and fulfil their dream.

▶ **Odysseus and Penelope: An Ordinary Marriage** – An entertaining novel by the classicist Inge Merkel (translated by Renate Latimer) that retells the myth from an unusual perspective

▶ **Captain Corelli's Mandolin** – the best selling novel by Louis de Bernières was also made into a film by John Madden (2001) starring Nicolas Cage and Penelope Cruz. The novel is set in Kefaloniá during the Second World War

▶ **The Magus** – by John Fowles (1966) is the ideal Greek holiday read. It is the story of a young Englishman who accepts a post as a teacher on a remote Greek island and is then drawn into a psychological adventure full of chilling twists and turns.

Well preserved 6th century mosaic floor in the Byzantine city of Nikópolis

lie right above a small beach, almost all have sea views. *Sivóta | on the small road above the bay | tel. 26 45 02 53 53 | www. sofia-studios.com| Budget*

INFORMATION

Available from the private travel agencies in Lefkáda, Nidrí and Vassilikí. For information about ferries, the best is *Borsalino Travel (Nidrí | on the thoroughfare close to the harbour | tel. 26 45 09 25 28 | borsalin @otenet.gr).*
The official island website is *www.lefkada. gr*

WHERE TO GO

KÁLAMOS (117 E–F 4–6) *(ﾩ F–G6)*
The small island (only 9 square miles but up to 785m/2575ft high in parts) has a population of 250 and is almost car-free. There are three tavernas in the main village of *Kálamos* and some small pebble

beaches in the hamlet of *Episkopí*. Regular connections to Mítikas (mainland) and in the summer some trips are organised to Kálamos from Lefkáda. You can overnight in a few private rooms.

KASTÓS (117 E–F 5–6) *(ﾩ F6–7)*
This tiny island (just 3 square miles with a population of 40) is entirely car-free. There are two tavernas and very basic accommodation in the community hall in the island's only village. Several small sandy beaches are accessible on foot. Regular ferry connections are available between the island and Mítikas (mainland). In the summer there are sometimes excursion boats from Lefkáda.

MEGANÍSI ★ (117 D4–5) *(ﾩ E5–6)*
Meganísi (pop. 500) is the largest of the islets between Léfkas and the mainland and is well worth a visit. The car ferry, which travels between Nidrí and the island several times daily, stops first at *Pórto*

Spília, with its short beach and taverna, before heading on to the main port of *Vathí.* A 15 minute walk on the island road leads from Vathí to the inland village of *Katoméri,* a further 60 minute walk leads to the picturesque village of *Spartochóri.* From there it is a short 10 minute walk to Pórto Spília. The most comfortable accommodation is the *Esperídes Resort (50 rooms | tel. 26 45 05 17 61 | www. esperides-resort.gr | Moderate)* between Pórto Spiliá and Spartochóri, there is also the family friendly hotel *Meganísi (35 rooms | tel. 26 45 05 12 40 | www. ionianislandholidays.com | Budget)* on the outskirts of Katoméri.

NIKÓPOLIS ★ (0) (𝄞 D–E1)

Impressive remains from antiquity are just 9km/5.5mi from Préveza on the mainland. The site is easily reached by bus from Léfkas. The trip is worthwhile even for those who are not particularly interested in archaeology.

Nikópolis was founded in 30 BC by Octavian, the future Roman Emperor Augustus, to commemorate his naval victory over Anthony and Cleopatra and it was settled until the 13th century. The city enjoyed its heyday during the early Byzantine period in the years between AD 500 and 600. Some of the foundation walls, stone carvings and mosaic floors of the basilicas dating to that era have been preserved. The most impressive of the remains are, however, the Byzantine city walls with its well preserved gates and towers. Even the amphitheatre is testimony to the size of the city, despite its destroyed terraces *(most of the excavations of the Byzantine city are open to the public, excavations of the ancientc city daily 8.30am–3pm | admission 2 euros).* In the small *excavation museum (Tue–Fri 8.30am–3pm, Sat/Sun 8am–3pm | admission 3 euros)* at the edge of the Doumetios Basilica there are Roman sculptures, glasses and coins. *Museum and excavations are on the main Préveza–Arta road | buses from Préveza*

PRÉVEZA (0) (𝄞 E2)

Préveza (pop. 15,000) is a small town surrounded by the sea on three sides, with a hint of the Orient. It is located at the mouth of the Ambracian Gulf, which stretches from here over 35km/22mi inland. In the 2002 an undersea tunnel was built under the mouth of the gulf connecting the town to the mainland.

On the other side of the gulf mouth a small fort marks the site of ancient *Actium,* which gave the sea battle its name. This decisive battle with Anthony and Cleopatra on the one hand and Octavian on the other hand, occurred in 31 BC, far out at sea.

A stroll through the main shopping street and the small market hall is worthwhile. Many of the houses date back to the 19th century; in the *Ágios Athanássios* church there are some murals. *Buses from Lefkáda to Préveza (21km/13mi away) run several times daily*

SKÓRPIOS (116–117 C–D4) (𝄞 E5)

The private island of the Onassis family is not open to the public. But you can view the island's private beaches and the rooftop of the houses by boat. On a trip around the island you imagine the lifestyle of the shipping magnate who lived here, first with the opera diva Maria Callas and then with Jackie Onassis.

VÓNITSA (0) (𝄞 F2)

A well preserved Venetian Turkish *castle* towers over the small town on the southern side of the Ambracian Gulf. *Castle is open to the public | buses from Lefkáda to Vónitsa (22km/14mi away) several times daily*

ZÁKYNTHOS

The Venetians called their southern-most property in the Ionian Sea *Fior di Levante*, 'the flower of the Levant'. The 157 square mile island was noted by the Italians for its fertility, its good wines, the lovely landscape and the aristocratic beauty of the island capital. Its beaches held little attraction to them.

However, today's visitors to the island come especially for the good sandy beaches. The most beautiful, those on the Bay of Laganás, have been sought out since time immemorial by sea turtles who visit to lay their eggs. During the 1980s tourism took root and a conflict of interest resulted in a bitter struggle between hotel devel-opers and nature conservation. On the one side there were those wanting more hotels, apartments, tavernas and shops along the beaches while the other side wanted the whole bay to be declared a national park and called for a tourism boycott of the island. Finally a compro-mise was reached.

The *Bay of Laganás* was declared a marine national park in December 1999. The beach of Sekaniá on the western side of the *Skopós Peninsula* is entirely off limits to the public. No boats may sail on the other beaches on the western side. In the remain-ing Bay of Laganás, the speed for motor boats is limited to six to eight knots; in

Photo: Typical swimming cove

The flower of the Levant: a fertile island caught between nature conservation and tourism development

the triangle between Laganás, Límni Kerioú and the small islet of Marathonísi boats may not anchor or birth. Bathing is still permitted on the tourist beaches. The national park administration also have information stands where people can educate themselves about the correct behaviour for welfare of the sea turtles.

Zákynthos is just as attractive for holiday-makers as it is for sea turtles. The centre of the island's capital is charming with large and small squares and its elongated position, between the sea and a low Bocháli range of hills ensures that the area stays contained. The bizarre rocks of the 492m/1614ft high summit of Mount Skopós create a prominent fixture on the horizon.

The island is clearly delineated, with a range of hills along the west and east

More boats than residents: the harbour village Ágios Nikólaos in the Bay of Skinári

coast. In the east the hills are green and low, in the west they rise up to a height of 756m/2480ft. The wide plain between them is intensively farmed and it is where the majority of island villages are located. In between the villages are country estates which are reminiscent of Tuscany with their beautiful gates and long driveways. In contrast to this lush fertility, large sections of the mountain area in the west only have woods or fields here and there. While the east coast is largely fringed by a narrow strip of beach, in the west the coast drops sharply into the sea. In some places there are still pristine sandy beaches such as Shipwreck Beach, which can only be reached by boat.

The approx. 39,000 Zákynthos locals are viewed as cheerful people. They celebrate carnival more intensively than any of other Ionian Islands – and they sing more often. Their typical songs are the more Italianate *kantádes* that have nothing in common with the folk music on the Aegean Islands and the mainland of Greece that are strongly influenced by the Orient. Even as a tourist you can learn *kantádes*: they are sung in many tavernas on the summer evenings.

SIGHTSEEING

INSIDER TIP AGALÁS
(122 C5) (∅ E18)

In the centre of the remote village a sign-post indicates the mile long way to the Venetian Wells (or *Andrónios Wells*); eleven well preserved cisterns from the Venetian era. They are ideally situated within a valley lined with vineyards *(open to the public; follow the the signs from the village and at the junction continue straight ahead until the asphalt ends).*

On the way to the cisterns, on the opposite side of the valley, you will see a cave opening in the rock; you can visit the cave on the way back. The double storey, *Spíleo tou Damianoú* cave is 200m from the car park, the beautiful route there is part of the attraction. In the village centre it is worth stopping off at the *Art Gallery (only open sporadically)* which is on the main road towards Kilioméno.

ÁGIOS NIKÓLAOS/SKINÁRI (122 B2) (*▯ D15*)

The little village on the Bay of Skinári only has 30 permanent residents, but is the second most important harbour on the island. This is where the excursion boats leave for the Blue Caves and Shipwreck Beach, and also where car ferries depart twice daily for Pessáda on Kefaloniá. The village sand and pebble beach is only a few hundred feet long.

ALIKÉS (122 C3) (*▯ E16*)

This coastal village is particularly popular with British holidaymakers. It is only sparsely developed and lies in on the edge of a disused salt flat right on a mile long, narrow sandy beach. In the evening there are often more horse-drawn carriages than cars on the road and the prices here are remarkably low. The small fishing port at the mouth of the river is especially charming. Approximately 150m/492ft upstream a six-arched Venetian era bridge spans the river.

INSIDER TIP ÁNO GERAKÁRI (123 D3) (*▯ E16*)

The courtyard of the *Ágios Nikólaos* church is the highest point of this inland village and it offers a good view over the island. It is best to leave your car at the village entrance as there is hardly any parking space in the village and at the top at the church.

ARGÁSSI (123 E4) (*▯ F17*)

Another holiday resort that is popular among British tourists, it stretches along a narrow, sandy beach and the main road on the Skopós Peninsula and also sprawls even further inland. From here the view

MARCO POLO HIGHLIGHTS

★ Blue Caves (Galázia Spílea)
A magical swim in a beautiful cave → p. 68

★ Bocháli
Pine trees within ruined medieval walls and fantastic views from the cliff → p. 68

★ Loúcha
Ancient village far from the beaten tourist track → p. 71

★ Shipwreck Beach (Navagíou)
A beautiful and isolated cove, with a shipwreck on the beach, which can only be reached by boat → p. 73

★ Zákynthos Museum
The Ionian Islands style of painting → p. 74

★ Varkaróla
Genuine Zakynthian *kantádes* sung every evening → p. 80

★ Apeláti
Modern guesthouse and taverna in the middle of olive trees and vineyards → p. 80

★ Olympia
Ancient sanctuary and sport complex – the place where the Olympic Games originated → p. 81

of Zákynthos Town is lovely. A three arched bridge from 1803, when the island was under British administration, confirms that Argássi was established well before the days of mass tourism. The ruined bridge is on the beach in front of the Xénos Kamára Beach Hotel (from the centre 30m behind the petrol station).

That Capri feeling: behind these rock arches are the Blue Caves of Zákynthos

BLUE CAVES (GALÁZIA SPÍLEA) ★ (122 B1) (🕮 D15)

The Blue Caves of Zákynthos are every bit as beautiful as their namesakes in Capri. You enter by boat, gliding through natural rock portals and bizarre formations into the crystal clear, blue and turquoise shimmering water of the grottos. Excursion boats to the caves depart regularly from Ágios Nikólaos/Skinári and from the pier below the lighthouse at Cape Skinári. There are also boat trips from Zákynthos Town and from Makrís Gialós.

BOCHÁLI ★ (123 D–E4) (🕮 F16)

The village on the elongated range of hills above the island capital is the ideal destination during the late afternoon and early evening. First you can visit the sprawling Venetian *fortress Bocháli (May–Oct daily 8am–2pm | admission 3 euros)*, which is almost completely overgrown with pine trees, forming a real forest. The outer walls and the gates are well preserved, but little remains of the other buildings such as the storerooms, churches and barracks. A café bar is strategically situated on the highest point of the fortress. *Free parking on the village street*
After visiting the fortress you can take a stroll to the village main square, which is on the steep slope of the hill range. The view over the town, the harbour and the Peloponnese is terrific. *Paid parking on the village street*

ÉXO CHÓRIA
(122 B3) (*ιΩ D16*)

The village *platía*, with its massive ancient plane tree, lies on the island's circular road. From here you can also reach over two dozen Venetian cisterns (just over a hundred feet away), which are in a field beside the main road towards Volimés. However, they are not as well preserved as those in Agalás.

GÍRI (122 B–C3) (*ιΩ D16*)

The highest village of the island is a particularly beautiful and unspoilt place. In its vicinity there are some windmill stumps and old threshing floors that testify to the once thriving grain farming industry. The earthquake of 1953 caused little damage in Gíri. The stonemason workshop at the village entrance is worth a visit, they carve Zakynthian stone reliefs out of limestone.

The *kafeníon* opposite the village church (dedicated to the Prophet Elijah) is like a small folkloric museum. The owner has set up numerous old farm implements in the courtyard of the farmhouse, including a grape press and a plough.

HELMÍ'S MUSEUM ●
(122 C4) (*ιΩ E16*)

This small private museum of natural history has more than 1500 exhibits – mainly specimens and fossils – that covers the island's past and present flora and fauna. *Agía Marína | daily 9am–6pm | www. museumhelmis.gr | admission 3 euros*

KALAMÁKI
(123 E4) (*ιΩ F17*)

Kalamáki has a sandy beach just as beautiful as that of the neighbouring Leganás, but it is far quieter. Hotels and guesthouses line the 200m/656ft village street and are also scattered in the area surrounding Kalamáki.

KALIPÁDO
(123 D3) (*ιΩ E16*)

The village is home to the island's largest private wine cellar: *Callínico (Mon–Sat 9am–8pm | signposted entrance on the main road from Zákynthos Town)*. Here you can not only enjoy a free wine tasting and buy wine, but you can also see a small exhibition that includes historic machinery, oak barrels, a wine press and the baskets in which the grapes used to be carried.

KAMBÍ ☀
(122 B4) (*ιΩ D17*)

Kambí is a village that is popular with tourists who come to enjoy the sunset and see the steep cliff. A large cross at this cliff commemorates the unknown number of left wing partisans who were thrown into the sea by their right wing opponents during the Greek Civil War in 1944. On the left hand side of the

LOW BUDGET

▶ In Zákynthos Town the best place for an inexpensive and delicious meal is the taverna *O Koúzis*. There is no menu and no outdoor seating, however they have a handful of fresh dishes daily from 4.50 euros, such as spaghetti with meat sauce or bean stew. *Mon–Fri noon–4pm | Odós Tertséti 54*

▶ The cheapest boat trips to the Blue Caves and Shipwreck Beach depart from the lighthouse at the most north-eastern tip. The boats leave for the caves every 10–15 minutes and to Shipwreck Beach several times a day (tour 7.50 euros).

From the village centre a road leads 2km/ 1.2mi to the lighthouse at ☀︎ *Cape Kerí*. The view from here over the 100m/328ft high cliff is magnificent. In the harbour village *Límni Kerioú* (123 D5) *(ⓜ E–F18)*, the diving centre of the island, is worth seeing for the ● *Herodotus Spring*, a source of both water and pitch. You are can collect some yourself. The short pebble beach of Límni Kerioú is ideal for a swim and every hour boat trips depart from the harbour to the cliffs and sea caves of Kerí.

MONASTERY OF ÁGIOS GEORGÍOU KREMNÓN (122 A2) *(ⓜ D15–16)*

Secluded monastery in a forest near to the cliff coast that looks just like a fortress. Until recently, only a lone monk still lived here, now the monastery is completely deserted. Its high walls hide a fortified tower with several 16th century pitch chutes and a beautiful monastery church with an 18th century baroque interior. Opposite the entrance to the monastery are four new bells in an olive tree, each labelled with the names of their donors.

MONASTERY OF ANAFONITRÍA (122 A3) *(ⓜ D16)*

Uninhabited monastery on the outskirts of Anafonitría village has its entrance through a massive 15th century tower gate that is overgrown with caper shrubs. The yellow Byzantine flag with the black double-headed eagle flies from the tower. The monastery church with frescoes from the 17th century is well preserved, and you can see the old oven and olive press used by the monks. The monastery was home to the island saint Dioissios in his last years as abbot. During this time he proved true Christian brotherly love: he offered his brother's murderer asylum in the monastery. *Cloisters open to the*

Last refuge: the fortified tower at the Monastery of Ágios Georgíou Kremnón

road that leads from the village up to the cross, are some shaft tombs from the Mycenaean period.

KERÍ/LÍMNI KERIOÚ

Kerí (123 D6) *(ⓜ E18)* is a picturesque mountain village (pop. 550) that is untouched by tourism, with quaint *kafenía*, that also double as grocery stores. The *Panagía tis Keriótissas* church has an impressive bell tower and a wooden carved iconostasis dating to 1745.

public, church daily 9am–1pm and 5pm–8pm | free admission

KORÍTHI
(122 B1) (*∅ D15*)

From the northernmost village of the island, a narrow asphalt road leads to *Cape Skinári* in the extreme north of the island. From the quay below the lighthouse there are short boat trips offered to the Blue Caves, also available in a glass bottom boat.

LAGANÁS
(123 D5) (*∅ F17*)

The main holiday resort destination of the island (along with neighbouring Kalamáki) is near to the airport flight path. Tourists using the beautiful sandy beach are a threat to the existence of the loggerhead sea turtle and as a result some of the large tour operators no longer offer Laganás as a destination. Nevertheless, the settlements keep spreading along the beach and deeper into the hinterland. The long main street that leads from the beach into the town is packed with bars and music clubs and even has the island's first McDonald's. There is a strong British presence, on Sundays restaurants offer Sunday roasts with Yorkshire pudding, in the bars guests are entertained with quiz sessions, karaoke and sport on big screens.

LITHÁKIA
(123 D5) (*∅ E–F17*)

The hamlet south of the island is worth a short stop to visit the ● *Aristeon Oive Press & Museum.* A family member is on hand to explain the long history of the company and the manufacturing process, and you can also do a tasting and purchase some of their organic oil. *Daily 8.30am–7pm*

LOÚCHA ★
(122 C4) (*∅ E17*)

This village, on the edge of a mountain valley, is only inhabited by a few elderly residents. It escaped damage in the 1953 earthquake and even its newer buildings have done little to change its authentic feel. It remains a good example of what Zakynthian villages looked like more than 50 years ago.

MORE THAN A 1000 NESTS

Loggerhead turtles *(Caretta caretta)* have been digging their nests on the sandy beaches of the Bay of Laganás since time immemorial. From June to August they come ashore in the evening to lay up to 120 ping pong ball size eggs before covering them with sand and heading back to the sea. A turtle can lay eggs up to three times during this time. After about 60 days the offspring hatch – again at night – and then immediately make their way to the sea. They orientate themselves by the starlight that is reflected on the water. Tourism however, threatens the turtles in various ways. Umbrellas stuck into the sand can destroy the eggs; nocturnal activities on the beach can prevent the mothers from laying their eggs. The newly hatched offspring may be guided in the wrong direction by lights close to the beach. They are then spotted by predators and snatched up or they dry out in the sun during the day.

The Panagía i Eleftherótria convent in Macherádo

MACHERÁDO
(122–123 C–D4) (*∅ E17*)

The church of *Agía Mávra (daily from sunrise to sunset | free admission)* in the large inland village of Macherádo (pop. 900) is the most important pilgrimage destination on the island. The church was destroyed by fire in 2007, but is now – depending on donations – undergoing renovations. The 16th century icon of St Mávra which was covered in a sheath of embossed silver in the 19th century survived intact and now miraculous powers are attributed to her. That is why she has numerous votive plaques around her, each one depicts what the faithful have prayed to her for assistance: a child, a house, healthy eyes or limbs, a healthy heart and more.

Above the village, to the left of the road to Kiloméno, is the INSIDERTIP *Panagía i Eleftherótria convent (daily 7am–noon and 4pm–dusk, when closed ring the bell).*

It was founded in 1961 and the abbey church has beautiful frescoes painted in the Byzantine style. In an adjoining room a nun shows stones from many biblical locations, such as the Sea of Galilee and the house of Mary in Nazareth. The first abbess of the convent gathered them herself on her travels.

INSIDERTIP NATIONAL MARINE PARK EXHIBITION CENTRE ●
(123 E5) (*∅ F17*)

The *Exhibition Centre* has some excellent displays of photographs and ceramic animals to show that there is so much more than just turtles to protect in the national marine park. *May, Sept, Oct daily 9am–5pm, June–Aug daily 9am–8pm | free admission | access from the main road between Vasilikós and Xirokástello, some 250m/820ft behind the windmill taverna, thereafter well signposted*

PIGADÁKIA
(122 C3) (ωω E16)

Spíros Vertzágio spent 15 years as the municipal leader of this small village in the hinterland of the seaside town of Alikés. The office was abolished in 2001 and he then opened his *Folk Museum (daily 9am–9pm | admission 3 euros | on the road to Alikés)* to display the antique island items – from household goods to agricultural equipment – that he had been collecting for more than 20 years. He also built a traditional straw hut, in the past these served as a resting place for the farmers during the harvest time and even as a place to stay overnight. Spíros also runs a traditional *taverna (Budget)* in the village centre, where he sells local produce such as currants, olive oil and wine.

The sound of splashing water is everywhere in the village as it has numerous springs, including a sulphurous spring under the altar of the small *chapel* opposite the taverna. A pot chained to the altar allows believers and the ill to draw from the spring. You can get to Pigadákia from Alikés either by horse and carriage or by miniature train (that runs on rubber wheels) that is also owned by Spíros *(the tour, including museum visit, is approx. 2 hours | fare 12.50 euros).*

PLÁNOS
(123 D3) (ωω F16)

The sprawling village has the sand and pebble beach, *Tsiliví Beach,* with its many hotels and taverna and is one of the most important resorts of the island. However, there is little in the way of sightseeing.

PÓRTO LIMNIÓNA
(122 B4) (ωω D17)

Getting into the water of the long, narrow fjord-like bay on the west coast is not very easy so after you have had your swim you can regain your strength at the *Pórto Limnióna Taverna (Moderate)* with lovely view out to sea.

PÓRTO RÓCHA (122 B5) (ωω D17)

You can reach the Bay of Pórto Rócha either from Pórto Limniónas or from the mountain village of Ágios León. For those brave enough, there is diving board about 5m/16ft above the water.

PÓRTO VRÓMI
(122 A3) (ωω C–D16)

It is believed that Mary Magdalene – according to the Gospel, she was the first to find that Jesus' grave was empty – came here on her way to Rome. Today the 10m/30ft long pebble beach has just a simple beach bar. The surrounding pines almost reach the water's edge. There are several excursion boats in the quay that do trips out to Shipwreck Beach *(2 hours incl. 1 hour swimming break | 15 euros/person).* Pedal boats are also rented out for rides on the fjord *(10 euros/ hour).*

ROMAS MANSION HOUSE
(123 E4) (ωω F16–17)

The house showcases how wealthy families lived on Zákynthos before the earthquake. The portraits, furniture, objet d'art, documents and the library however may not maybe not be worth the high price of admission for some. *Closed at the time of going to press, enquire about opening times in town | admission 5 euros | Zákynthos Town | Odós Loúka Karrér 19 | www.romas.gr*

SHIPWRECK BEACH (NAVAGÍOU) ★
(122 A2) (ωω C15–16)

Images of this beautiful beach are often used to promote Greece all over the world *(see p. 125).* The remote cove's white, sandy beach is only accessible by boat and it lies at the foot of a steep cliff – and in the middle of the beach is the wreck of the freighter that ran aground in the 1970s. The shimmering water is a deep turquoise, on some days with swirls of white.

You can get to Shipwreck Beach by boat from Pórto Vromí; however your dream photo can only be taken from the edge of the cliff. To get there you have to drive from the Monastery of Ágios Georgíou Kremnón northwards, after 200m turn left and go a further 1200m to the restaurant. There – behind some stalls selling drinks, herbs and honey – is a small viewing platform that juts out over the abyss, which is very reminiscent of the Skywalk over the Grand Canyon. From here you have a perfect view of *Shipwreck Beach*.

SKOPÓS PENINSULA
(123 E–F 4–5) (*G17*)

The peninsula in the south-east of the island capital has been named after Mount Skopós (492m/1614ft) which towers above it. The north of the peninsula is lined with many small bays with sand and pebble beaches and only very few hotels and apartment blocks. In the south of the peninsula is the Bay of Laganás with miles of sandy beaches. However, the beaches form part of the nesting area for the loggerhead turtles and should therefore be avoided.

SOLOMÓS MUSEUM
(123 E4) (*F16–17*)

The most important poet of the Ionian Islands, Dioníssios Solomós (1798–1857) and his fellow poet Andréas Kálvos (1792–1869) are both buried here and the ground floor is their mausoleum. Through his work –which includes the text of the Greek national anthem – Dioníssios Solomós helped the Greek vernacular to gain literary recognition. The following

words are engraved on his tomb 'pand' anikta, pand' ágripna, ta matja tis psichís mou' (always open, always mindful, the eyes of my soul). *Closed at time of going to press, enquire about opening times in town | admission 4 euros | Zákynthos Town | Platía Agíu Márkou*

VÓLIMES
(122 B2) (*D15*)

The rambling mountain village in the north of the island looks like a large market during the summer. Everywhere along the roadside there are sellers with 'genuinely handmade' embroidered cloths and decorated covers. A few of them actually are the handiwork of Zakynthian women – but the majority of the wares come from workshops on the mainland and are not handmade at all.

ZÁKYNTHOS MUSEUM ★ ●
(123 E4) (*F16–17*)

The museum provides a detailed overview of the history of painting on the Ionian Islands and especially of the works of the so-called Ionian School of the 17–19th century, which was strongly influenced by Italian painting. A relief model and historical photos show what the town looked like before the earthquake in 1953. *Tue–Sun 9am–2pm | admission 3 euros | Zákynthos Town| Platía Solomoú*

ZÁKYNTHOS TOWN
(123 E4) (*F16–17*)

MAP INSIDE BACK COVER

After the earthquake of 1953, Zákynthos Town (pop. 11,000) had to be completely rebuilt. Fortunately the result is not an ugly town in the style of the 1950s, but a good mix of historical reconstruction and appealing new buildings. The only sightseeing options though are the museums, but there are a few interesting churches.

Right on the coast is the large Platía Solomoú and the church of the patron saint of seafarers, the *Ágios Nikólaos*. It was built in 1560 with funding by the local fishermen's guild. On the Platía Agíou Márkou with its many cafés, is the *San Marcus* church right next to the Solomós Museum, and in summer a Roman Catholic mass takes place here every Sunday at in town, dedicated to the island saint *Dioníssios*. This church was also repainted in the traditional Byzantine style in the 1980s. Parts of the frescoes depict scenes from the life and work of the saint, who was born on Zákynthos in 1547 and died here in 1622. Especially beautiful are the frescoes on the western wall that represent the history of creation; they were

Dominating the waterfront landscape of Zákynthos: Dioníssios church (right) and campanile

7pm. The painting above the altar is said to be by Titian or one of his students.

If you walk a few steps east from the Platía Agíou Márkou, you will come across the *Mitrópolis,* the town's cathedral. It is decorated with magnificent frescoes in the traditional Byzantine style. Continue from the Mitrópolis towards the sea, turn left at the first intersection and you will see the very beautiful INSIDER TIP portal of the *Kiría ton Ángelon* church *dating back to* 1687.

At the western end of the coastal road is the largest and most important ● church done in 1990 and have a naïve style similar to works by Henri Rousseau. The western facade is adorned with modern mosaics depicting the patron saints of three Ionian Islands: Saint Spyridon of Corfu, Saint Gerássimos of Kefaloniá and Saint Dioníssios of Zákynthos. The remains of the island's saint are particularly revered and lie in a silver sarcophagus. The magnificent sarcophagus stands in a side chapel to the right of the chancel *(daily 4am–noon and 5pm–9.30pm)*. In the adjoining building is the island's *Bishop's Palace*.

When you return to the town centre, take Odós Tertséti street and on your left hand side you will find a small piece of land where the island's synagogue once stood. It was founded in 1489 by the Jewish community but was destroyed in 1953 by

race you overlook the hills of the island. Host Andónis Maroúdas offers different freshly prepared dishes; the ingredients change daily so there is no menu. His wine house wine comes from his own vineyard. Occasionally *kantádes* are played

Kókkinos Vráchos, (red rocks) is most elegant coffee house in Zákynthos Town

the earthquake. Two *memorials (Odós Tertséti 44)* commemorate the island's Orthodox bishop and the mayor of Zákynthos at time of the German occupation during the Second World War. They bravely resisted the Nazi order to supply a list of their Jewish fellow citizens, and in so doing saved them from evacuation to the German extermination camps.

FOOD & DRINK

ALITZERÍNI
(122 C4) (*Ø E17*)
The taverna, in a traditional two-storey Zakynthian farmhouse, is well known by all the island locals. From the small ter-

in the evening. *June–Sept daily from 7pm otherwise only Fri–Sun from 7pm | Kilioméno | on the road from the village centre to Macherádo | Expensive*

GALAXY (122 A2) (*Ø D16*)
A very popular taverna that is great for lunch, with a wide selection of dishes *Anafonítrias | in the village centre | Budget*

KÉFALOKOLÓNNA (122 C3) (*Ø D16*)
The host family serves their traditional dishes, with fresh ingredients from the region, in a courtyard covered in grape vines. If they feel in the mood then the host and his son sometimes sing the best *kantádes. Girí | on the outskirts of town*

(from the car park go to the end of the village street) | Budget

KÓKKINOS VRÁCHOS
(123 E4) (*Ø F16–17*)

The most elegant coffee house in the town. Even if you sit outside on the square or under the arcade, you must make sure you can see into the beautifully maintained interior. *Zákynthos Town | Platía Solomoú (in the library building)* | Moderate

LA STORIA (122 B2) (*Ø D15*)

A fish taverna ideally situated on the beach, aside from fresh fish they also serve grilled octopus and *astakómakaronáda*, noodles with langoustine. *Ágios Nikólaos | on the coastal road* | Expensive

PEPPERMINT (123 E4) (*Ø F17*)

Simple, but modern restaurant serving sophisticated cuisine, such as pork fillet in an orange cognac sauce or veal fillet with caramelised onions. *Argássi | at the northern town entrance* | Expensive

INSIDER TIP PÓRTO ROÚLIS
(123 D3) (*Ø E–F16*)

Host Dioníssos and his wife Katína run one of the most authentic taverna on the island. The terrace is right next to the sea ocean; the small pebble beach in front of the taverna is also good for swimming. You will be served fish caught that very morning by Dioníssos caught himself, as well as meat from the island. During the high season one or two baked dishes are also available. *Drossía | 300m north of Hotel Tsámis* | Moderate

INSIDER TIP PORTOKÁLI
(123 E4) (*Ø F17*)

The most unusual restaurant of the island, a lounge bar, that serves both cocktails and a wide selection of dishes. The colourful decor is as unusual as the menu. The walls are often decorated with contemporary art and there are occasionally live concerts and guest appearances by British DJs. *Argássi | at the northern town entrance | www.portokalion.gr* | Moderate

TO FANÁRI TU KERIOÚ ☼
(122 C6) (*Ø E18*)

Well maintained taverna high above the cliff with dazzling views. Host Stamátis Livéris is actually a construction engineer, but likes to indulge his love of the culinary arts. Some of his specialities include rabbit and chicken stuffed with liver, rice, cheese and vegetables as well as pork belly stuffed with vegetables. Most of the dishes are prepared in a wood-fired oven. *Kerí | 1.5km/1mi outside the town, some 150m from the lighthouse* | Moderate

INSIDER TIP TO KAFENÍO TIS LOÚCHAS
● ☺ (122 C4) (*Ø E16–17*)

A retired Zakynthian teacher maintains the island traditions in the quiet village Loúcha. His *kafeníon* is open all year round, and in addition to coffee and soft drinks, he also serves regional products like organically grown salad, tomatoes, feta cheese and fried chips from freshly cut potatoes. Of course, the olive oil he uses also comes from the island and the fresh, cold water is from a nearby spring. In fine weather guests sit on the garden terrace under vines, on cooler days in a heated, wooden conservatory. *Loúcha | at the village church* | Budget

SHOPPING

ÉLLINON GÉFSIS
(123 E4) (*Ø F16–17*)

The attractively decorated 'Greek taste' offers culinary delights and cosmetics from all over Greece, including ☺ numerous organically grown products. *Zákynthos Town | Odós Alex. Roma 13*

HANNE MI'S CERAMIC ART STUDIO ● (123 F5) (*ɷ G17*)

The Norwegian artist Hanne Mi, who also worked for the National Marine Park, produces ceramic and earthenware of high quality: tiles and fountains, bowls and vases, cups, plates, egg cups, frames – and of course decorative turtles. She also offers two-hour *pottery classes (Tue and Sat 10am–noon | 20 euros)* as well as private lessons. *Vassilikós | on the main road before the turn-off to Porto Roma Beach | www.ceramichannemi.com*

A Greek siren in stone: mermaid statue at Banana Beach

MANTOLÁTO (123 E4) (*ɷ F16–17*)

Large selection of culinary specialities, especially sweets. *Zákynthos Town | Odós El. Venizélou/Odós Defsíla*

POTTERY OF ZÁKYNTHOS (123 E4) (*ɷ F16–17*)

Simple ceramics from an island pottery studio. *Zákynthos Town | Odós Alex. Róma 20*

SPORTS & BEACHES

Numerous beaches line the south and east coast of the island. On the north and west coast on the other hand, there are only a few beaches, and almost all of them are only accessible by boat. The following is a selection of the best beaches, those worth a trip from other parts of the island.

BANÁNA BEACH ☼ (123 F5) (*ɷ G17*)

On the Skopós Peninsula this dead straight sandy beach is over half a mile long and is still largely undeveloped. There are sun loungers under palm thatched umbrellas and sweepings views over the sea to the Peloponnese. In the eastern part there are low scrub dunes. In the western part, called *Ionian Beach*, there are also showers available. *Buses from Argássi and Zákynthos Town stop on the main road about 300m/985ft from the beach*

GERÁKAS BEACH ☺ (123 F5) (*ɷ G17–18*)

This beautiful sandy beach is where sea turtles and tourists try to coexist. Beach use is only allowed during the day and conservationists make sure that the correct behaviour is observed. There are designated areas for bathing, umbrellas may only rest on the sand (not pushed into it) and there are no taverna right into the hinterland.

KAMÍNIA BEACH
(123 F5) (*M G17*)

The almost 130m/427ft rough sand and fine gravel beach has some Tamarisk trees that provide shade. Sun loungers and umbrellas are available on the green lawn and are even provided for free to beach bar guests. There are even some swing hammocks. *Buses stop on the main road about 200m/656ft from the beach*

MAKRÍS GIALÓS
(122 B2) (*M D15*)

Well maintained gravel beach that has some sun loungers and umbrellas rentals. It lies about 800m/2624ft south of the scenic hamlet of *Mikró Nisí*, which is built in an idyllic location on a flat ledge that protrudes into the sea.

INSIDER TIP MINIATURE GOLF
(123 E4) (*M F17*)

One of the most idiosyncratic miniature golf courses in Europe is the work of one a local. The two 18 hole courses include replicas of Stonehenge, the Golden Gate Bridge, the Statue of Liberty, the Irish Blarney Castle, the Leaning Tower of Pisa and many other world famous landmarks. In the evening, the course is attractively lit. *Daily 10am–2am | Argássi | www.worldtourminigolf.com*

MOTOR BOATS (123 D5) (*M F18*)

If you rent a motor boat (no licence required) in *Límni Kerioú*, you can cross the Bay of Laganás or circle the turtle island of Marthonísi. *40 euros/3hours.*

MOUNTAIN BIKING & HIKING

Bicycle rentals and guided mountain bike tours are offered by *Podilatadiko (Zákynthos Town | Platía Agíou Pávlou/Odós Koutouzi 88 | tel. 26 95 02 44 34 | www.podilatadiko.com)*. The longest tour is 120km/75mi around the island, the most strenuous is a 35km/22mi long crossing of the island mountains. Guided hikes are also arranged. Dates and prices are subject to demand and the number of participants.

PÓRTO ZÓRRO BEACH
(123 E–F4) (*M G17*)

The small sandy beach cove on the Skopós Peninsula gets its appeal from some of the large off shore rocks that are covered in lush vegetation. There is a taverna and various water sport activities. *Buses stop on the main road 250m/820ft from the beach*

SAN NICOLAS BEACH
(123 F5) (*M G17*)

A 300m/984ft sandy beach on Skopós Island that has sun lounger rentals, showers and water sports activities. In the north the beach is bordered by the *Saint Nicholas chapel* on a low, rocky promontory, which is especially lovely at dusk. *Free shuttle buses in the morning from Laganás (Hotel Laganás), Kalamáki (main intersection) and Argássi (Hotel Mimósa)*

ENTERTAINMENT

O ADELFÓS TU KÓSTA/KOSTAS' BROTHER TAVERNA
(123 F4) (*M G17*)

An idyllically situated garden taverna where *kantádes* are sung in the evenings on weekends. Specialities of the house are rabbit and *kokorás ragú* a chicken ragout with lots of vegetables. *Open during carnival, Easter and June–Sept Fri–Sun from 8pm, July/August also on other days | below the main road between Banána Beach and Ionion Beach | Moderate*

SARAKÍNA (123 D5) (*M F17*)

Costumed locals perform Greek dances every evening from 7pm–9pm in the large taverna next to the ruins of the historic manor of Sarakína, they also sing *kantádes*. The event even ends with a Greek party where the guests may dance along. A free yellow minibus shuttles between the restaurant and various stops in Laganás from 6.30–10pm. *2km/1.2mi from the centre of Laganás on the road to Pantokrátoras, clearly signposted | tel. 26 95 05 16 06 | Expensive*

VARKARÓLA ★ ●
(123 E4) *(ℳ F16–17)*
You will hear Zakynthian *kantádes* every evening in this taverna on the harbour road. Often guests with their own instruments and good voices join in resulting in spontaneous international music evenings. They have a selection of snacks to eat, and to drink ☺ they serve a dry, organically grown Verdea wine from the vineyards of host Yiannis and his brother Kóstas. *Daily from noon, music from approx. 9pm | Zákynthos Town | Odós Lomvárdou 30 | Moderate*

WHERE TO STAY

APELÁTI ★ (123 D6) *(ℳ E18)*
A modern house that doubles as a restaurant and affordable guesthouse on a small plateau in the south-west of the island surrounded by vineyards and olive trees. The very friendly proprietress, Mrs Dénia, rents out five rooms with bathrooms; the women of the family prepare good home-style cooking in the kitchen. Vegetables, wine, goat and rabbit that mostly come from their own farm. *Kerí | off the main road from Límni Kerioú to Kerí | tel. 26 95 03 33 24 | Budget*

INSIDER TIP ARCHONTIKÓ VILLAGE
(122 C3) *(ℳ E16)*
A stately former olive oil press, flour mill and wine cellar dating back to 1846 that has been restored and now forms the core of a small hotel complex with six holiday cottages and seven simply furnished apartments, in a lush garden with a large swimming pool and a poolside café. *Katastári | tel. 26 95 08 30 35 | www.archontikovillage. com | Moderate*

BALCONY HOTEL
(123 D3) *(ℳ F16)*
Modern hotel built in the traditional *Zákynthos* style, on a promontory overlooking the Bay of Tsílivi. Steps lead you down to the sandy beach. *34 rooms | Tsilíví | 500m/1640ft from the village centre on the road to Zákynthos | tel. 26 95 02 86 38 | www.zakynthos-net.gr/balcony | Budget*

INSIDER TIP DAPHNE'S STUDIOS
(123 F5) *(ℳ G17)*
Only 100m/328ft from Pórto Róma Beach the seven ground floor apartments and four holiday houses of Dionýsis Tsilimígras and his Swedish wife María are set in a quiet, geen oasis on the edge of a forest. On the terraces of the sprawling grounds there are loungers and hammocks and the kitchens are well above average. Four mountain bikes are available for use at no additional charge. *Vassilikós | Pórto Róma | tel. 26 95 03 53 19 | www.daphnes-zakynthos.com | Moderate*

DIÁNA (123 E4) *(ℳ F16–17)*
You cannot stay more central than in this modern hotel on the Platía Agíiou Márkou. *51 rooms | Zákynthos Town | Platía Agíou Márkou | tel. 26 95 02 85 47 | www.diana hotels.gr | Expensive*

INSIDER TIP MÝLOS ☼
(122 B1) *(ℳ D15)*
A very romantic option with wonderful views are these two well-equipped converted windmills on the cliff directly above

Something unusual: holiday accommodation in the Mýlos stone windmills on Cape Skinári

the Blue Caves. There are steps leading down to a small sun terrace at the sea and there is a taverna 200m away. *2 apartments (2–4 persons) | Cape Skinári | tel. 26 95 03 11 32, mobile tel. 69 72 05 57 11 | www.potamitisbros.gr | Expensive*

PÓRTO KOÚKLA BEACH
(123 D5) *(ₐ F18)*

Small hotel set in a green area on a long, narrow sandy beach south of the islet Ágios Sóstis, with a host who loves to sing! Turtles are not endangered on this beach. *35 rooms | Lithákia | signposted access off the Laganás-Kerí road | tel. 26 95 05 23 93 | www.pavlos.gr | Moderate*

INFORMATION

TOURISM POLICE (123 E4) *(ₐ F16–17)*
Zákynthos Town | Odós Lombardoú 62 | tel. 26 95 02 73 67
Best island website: www.zanteweb.gr

FERRY CONNECTIONS

All year round car ferries travel several times daily between Zákynthos Town and Killíni (Pelopennes). *Mon–Sat first ferry to Killíni 5.30am, Sun 8am, last ferry from Killíni daily 9.30pm | ferry price 9 euros*
From May until October a ferry travels twice daily between Ágios Nikólaos/Skinári and Pessáda (Kefaloniá).

WHERE TO GO

OLYMPIA ★ (0) *(ₐ 0)*
MAP INSIDE BACK COVER
The place where the Olympic Games originated is an easy day trip. You can their book it as a boat-bus tour through a travel agency or go there on your own by car. From Zákynthos to the ferry port of Killíni takes about 90 minutes, from there it is another 75km/47mi on a well maintained road to Olympia.

40 columns once supported the roof of the Temple of Hera in Olympia

The Olympic Games took place for more than 1100 years in the ancient Greek sanctuary of Olympia. They started in 776 BC and were held for the last time around AD 400, before they were once again revived 1500 years later in their modern form.

Tour: The best place to start your tour, and in order to understand Olympia, is the entrance to the *Temple of Zeus*. You will easily spot the temple with its three tiered base and the many massive column remains that are toppled around it. This temple was the religious centre of the sanctuary. On the almost 28m/92ft wide and over 64m/210ft long upper step of the substructure there once stood 36 Doric columns, each over 10m/33ft high. Completed in 457 BC, the main structure of the temple was built out of limestone and surrounded a windowless *cella*, with a doorway in the east. In its interior, in mystical semi-darkness, stood one of the seven wonders of the ancient world: a 13m/43ft high hollow statue of Zeus made from gold, silver, ivory and precious

stones. It was the work of Phidias, who also had a hand in the creation of the adornments for the Parthenon Temple in the Athenian Acropolis. On the western opposite side of the temple are the high brick walls of a 5th century *basilica* which was built in the place where Phidias' workshop once stood.

South of the workshop, is the *Leonidaion*, the lodgings guests of honour, which was embellished in Roman times by a large, still identifiable water basin. North of the *workshop of Phidias*, is the largest 3rd century BC *Palaistra* with still visible rows of columns where the wrestling matches were carried out. In the northern part of the courtyard is the preserved grooved pavement that gave the wrestlers more grip and stability.

Looking north from the Temple of Zeus you will see the *Temple of Hera*, which has a number of different types of columns. The portico column drums have differing styles and their capitals are also different, one of the pillars has only 16 instead of the

date 45 000 spectators in the surrounding well-preserved mud seats. Only the referees sat on stone benches. The stone start and finish lines can still clearly be seen at both ends of the stadium.

On the way back to the entrance of the excavation area lie the remains of the *Philippeion*: two circular foundations that once supported a round temple. The Macedonian King Philip II donated it in 338 BC, his son Alexander the Great completed it.

North of the Philippeion you can see the remains of the *Prytaneion*, where the Olympic champions were entertained. On the other side of the road lie the scant remains of the 3rd century BC *gymnasium* where the Olympians trained on an elongated space surrounded by colonnades *(May–Sept daily 8am–7pm, Oct–April 8am–sundown (Easter Friday 8am–noon), 1 Jan, 25 March, Easter Sunday, 1 May, 25/26 Dec closed | admission 6 euros, combined ticket with Archaeological Museum 9 euros).*

In the *Archaeological Museum* opposite the archaeological site holds some of the greatest art treasures of Greece. These include the marble sculptures from the pediment area of the Temple of Zeus and its metopes of marble panels with relief plates, a large bronze horse dating from around 800 BC, the chalice of the sculptor Phidias and a Roman statue of a bull. The two most famous statues are the Hermes of Praxiteles and Nike the goddess of victory, both works from the Classical era *(May–Oct, Mon noon–7pm, Tue–Sun 8am–7pm, Oct–April Mon 10.30am–5pm, Tue–Sun 8.30am–3pm).*

The displays in the *Museum of the History of the Olympic Games* include ancient sporting equipment while the *Museum of the History of Excavations* show the work of archaeologists *(opening time as per the Archaeological Museum | free admission).*

usual 20 flutings. This indicates that the temple (built around 600 BC) originally had wooden columns, which were replaced by stone ones over the centuries, each corresponding to the style of the time.

To the one side of the Temple of Hera, is the *Nyphaeum* (a semi-circular fountain from the Roman era) with a *terrace* where an array of treasuries representing the eleven Greek city states once stood. This was where they held their most valuable votive offerings to Zeus. Numerous votive offerings of other city states were set up around the sacred precinct.

The treasuries terrace ends at the *entrance to the stadium*, originally covered by a vaulted roof. A part of it was reconstructed by archaeologists. Right at the entrance you can see the long stretch of the foundations of the *Echo Hall*, a long lobby where the announcements were made, that provided protection from the rain and the midday sun.

The ancient *Olympic stadium* is a surprisingly simple building. It could accommo-

TRIPS & TOURS

The tours are marked in green in the road atlas, the pull-out map and on the back cover

1 ONCE AROUND ZÁKYNTHOS

Length of the sightseeing roundtrip: approx. 170km/ 105mi starting and ending in Zákynthos Town. It is best to collect your rental vehicle the evening before so that you can set out early in the morning. And do not forget your swimming gear because there are some beautiful beaches along the way!

The first destination of the trip is the pitch spring in Límni Kerioú → p. 70. After you have collected your souvenir sample of tar it is off to the first real pleasure of the day, the  view from the Kerí → p. 70 lighthouse on the scenic cliff coast. On the way back to the island interior you should stop for a coffee in one of the rustic general stores on the village square in Kerí, where you can also support the village's economy by stocking up on food and ice-cold mineral water for the journey.

A further 2.5km/1.5mi and you turn left to the peaceful mountain village of Agalás → p. 66. From Kilioméno the road continues to Ágios Léon, where at the start of the village a narrow road leads to the quiet villages of Loúcha → p. 71 and Gíri → p. 69. Here you are right off the

Beaches, monasteries and villages: get to know the most beautiful aspects of four Ionian Islands with these easy day trips

tourist track and can enjoy a snack in a truly authentic Greek atmosphere. Afterwards pay a visit to the prominent cross above Kambí → p. 69, the view from up here over the rugged cliffs inspires one to whip out the sketchbook – or at least the camera.

In Anafonítrias you should first travel to the Monastery of Anafonitría → p. 70 set in the midst of lush greenery, before head-

ing down into the village itself for lunch. After the Monastery of Ágios Georgíou Kremnón → p. 70, which is somewhat tucked away in the forest, turn left towards Shipwreck Beach → p. 73. The beach is every bit as picturesque when seen from above as it is from the water. If you feel like doing some shopping – very undemanding – you can do so in Vólimes → p. 74.

At the lighthouse of Skinári → p. 67 you are at the northernmost tip of the island. From here you can take a boat trip to the Blue Caves → p. 68, you will need to set aside at least an hour. Via Koríthi → p. 71 and Ágios Nikólaos → p. 67 the road continues on to Mikró Nisí, where you can take a dip at Makrís Gialós → p. 79. A longer stop is worthwhile in Alikés → p. 67. The village church Áno Gerakári → p. 67 sits up on a hill and

2 SOUTHERN KEFALONIÁ

The journey around Énos – the highest summit of the Ionian Islands – includes numerous flower-filled villages, good beaches, some historical sites, a small lake and a large monastery. Length of the roundtrip from Argostóli: approx. 90km/56mi, including Énos approx. 130km/81mi.

Testimony of an ancient culture: Mycenaean tomb dating back to 1350 BC in Tzanáta

overlooks large parts of the island. After admiring the view you return via the lively seaside resorts of Plános and Tsilívi in the island's capital.

From Argostóli follow the signs to the airport. From here you go through prosperous and well-maintained villages such as Svoronáta and Metaxáta → p. 45.

Both Katélios Beach and Kamínia Beach → p. 48 are worth a detour before you reach the seaside village of Skála → p. 47 and the remains of an ancient Roman villa. Then the trip follows the coast to the ferry port of Póros → p. 46, where you can take a detour to the island's oldest monastery Moní tis Panagías tis Atroú. Close by is one of the oldest historical monuments of the island, the Mycenaean tomb at Tzanáta → p. 47.

Now it gets more isolated, there is not a single village for the next 18km/12mi. The road passes between the 1628m/5340ft high massif of Énos and the 1078m/3536ft high Kókkini Rachí and the small, reed fringed Avíthos Lake → p. 41, ideal for a picnic. Another lovely place for a picnic is the ruins of Ancient Sámi high above the seaside resort of Sámi → p. 46, from where the ferries also leave for the neighbouring island of Ithaca. If you still have some time, a worthwhile option is a return trip to Argostóli with a detour to the Monastery of Ágios Gerássimos → p. 43 (the largest on the island) and wine tasting in the cellar of Robóla. Mountaineers and hikers can now drive another 15km/9mi on a paved road up to the antenna system just below the summit of Énos → p. 42 where several suitable signposted hiking trails begin.

3 KEFALONIÁ'S BEAUTIFUL NORTH

Numerous of natural attractions, idyllic villages and fantastic beaches await visitors to the north of the island. Length of the roundtrip from Sámi: approx: 100km/62mi.

From Sámi the road follows the coast to the small seaside village Agía Efímia, where it turns inland to Divaráta on the other side of the island. Here you have a magnificent view of the bay and the unspoilt sand and pebble beach of Mírtos, with an asphalt road winding down to the beach. This is the ideal spot for a swim here. Next up is an extensive coffee break in the historic village of Ássos → p. 41 with its picturesque bay and Venetian castle. Back on the road the trip heads north to Fiskárdo → p. 42 with its scenic townscape and bay lined with yachts of all sizes.

While tourists crowd other resorts, the inland village of Mesovouniá remains a quiet and unspoilt. The next few villages on the narrow winding road, such as Plagiá, Kariá and Komitáta, all look desolated outside of the summer months, because only a few of the elderly inhabitants still farm here. If you are lucky, you will find an open village kafenío where the few guests and the hosts will be more than happy to welcome a foreign visitor.

Then you will be at the coast again in Agía Efímia. Just before Sámi, take a magical boat ride in the stalactite caves of Melissáni → p. 45 (closed in the morning) before enjoying a final sundowner or an early dinner at the taverna Karavómilos → p. 43 with a spring where the children can fed the ducks.

4 SEA KAYAK TRIP IN KEFALONIÁ

Kefaloniá still offers secluded beaches and impressive coastlines. The best way to explore them is by kayak on a good guided daytrip in a small group. Single and double boats are available and there are regular breaks to go swimming and snorkelling. More than ten different day trips are available. Highly recommended is the tour from the Argostóli lighthouse to the beach of Miniés. Duration: approx. 5 hours, 60 euros incl. lunch. *Seakayaking*

Kefaloniá| Trapesáki | mobile tel. 69 34 01 04 00 | www.seakayakingkefalonia-greece.com

The tour is suitable for all age groups and also for novice kayakers. It starts at 9.30am at the lighthouse at the tip of the Lássi Peninsula → p. 44, which is shaped like an ancient Greek round temple. After a short introduction to kayaking it's time to set off. The first section takes you past caves and small, secluded coves. You can paddle into many caves and will be amazed at how big they are.

After 90 minutes of paddling you will have the first stop, a break to go swimming, snorkeling and to enjoy a small snack. Then the trip continues on past the beach of Makrís Giálos → p. 48 with its hotels and imposing limestone cliffs. The coastline slowly becomes a little more remote and after about 40 minutes you will reach a wonderful INSIDER TIP *white, sandy beach* that is only accessible by boat. The incredible colour of the water makes you feel as though you are in the Caribbean. A tasty lunch awaits you on the beach and you will also have enough time for a swim and snorkel. Then you set off to paddle into the last cave and 20 minutes later you will reach the beach of Miniés north of the airport.

5 A LONG DAY ON LÉFKAS

In order to see all of Léfkas in one day, you will need to get up early and leave before 8am. Length of the roundtrip from Lefkáda: approx. 160km/99mi.

Your trip starts at the ☆ outskirts of Lefkáda with a panoramic view of the town, the lagoon and across to the mainland. At the end of the climb you may just arrive at worship time in the Monastery of Faneroménis → p. 55. It is lovely to spend a few minutes in the lush green garden and listen to the Orthodox liturgy, without disturbing the devout.

The road soon descends down to the coast and passes the long beaches of Ágios Nikítas → p. 54. The route travels past the very scenic mountain villages of Drimónas and Exanthía to Komilió, where the road to the Lefkáta Peninsula → p. 56 starts. Travel the road up to Cape Doukáto → p. 56 and then take a swimming break at Pórto Katsíki → p. 56 which is very popular and can be crowded in midsummer.

Return to the main road, you now drive to Vassilikí → p. 57 with its nice cafés and tavernas in the harbour and wide range of water sports on the beach. A detour into the hilly interior brings you to the mountain village Sívros. Shortly thereafter, if time allows, you can take a detour to ☆ Póros with its beautiful views and historical village centre. The pebble beach far below the village is ideal for a cooling swim on a hot day. The island's ring road soon takes you to the Bay of Vlichó → p. 57 and then the major seaside resort of Nidrí → p. 56, the starting point for many boat excursions to some beautiful spots.

After having yourself photographed with the statue of Aristotle Onassis, the drive heads back into the interior. The fantastic ☆ INSIDER TIP panoramic views of the Bay of Vlichó, which in the late afternoon is visited by countless yachts, the small islands east of Léfkas and the mountainous mainland are among the most beautiful that Greece has to offer. You then pass through the sleepy mountain village of Vafkéri with its authentic taverna and then further on to the large mountain village Kariá → p. 54, where you can dine well in the pleasant village square. From there it is only 15km/9mi back to the island capital.

6 ON ODYSSEUS' ISLAND

Most visitors come to Ithaca to follow in the footsteps of Odysseus. You can visit hike to quite a few destinations around Vathí that are linked to the Homeric epic. The walks themselves are worth it as you will get a real feel for the beauty of the island. Roundtrip from Vathí: approx. 18km/12mi.

follow the route that Odysseus took to hide the treasure that he brought with him on his boat. From the caves you can take the signposted path to an ancient sarcophagus and from there back to Vathí.

Now you can take the path to the Arethoúsa Spring → p. 34. From the spring the narrow route leads a further 900m on the Marathias plateau to where – according to legend – Eumaeus, Odysseus' swineherd, grazed his pigs. You can also see a gun emplacement from the Second World War. A signpost indicates the path to the

One encounters Odysseus everywhere: such as this statue of the hero in Vathí

From Vathí you can walk the coastal road to the Bay of Dexiá → p. 34, or take the local bus, and take a swim on one of the beaches where Odysseus also waded into the water. From here you can now head to the Grotto of the Nymphs → p. 35 and

cave where the faithful herdsman supposedly lived.

To return you have to backtrack but thanks to the impressive coastal panorama and the intense fragrance of herbs, the route is never boring.

SPORTS & ACTIVITIES

The islands of this region have fewer sporting activities than on many other Greek islands. Zákynthos is famous for its many good dive sites, Léfkas is regarded as a hot spot for windsurfers and cyclists will feel at home on Kefaloniá and Léfkas.

BOAT TRIPS

The largest selection of boat trips is offered on Léfkas. The ● *Nidri Star I* departs almost daily from Nidrí to the beach of Pórto Katsíki, then on to Fiskárdo on Kefaloniá and to Ithaca. On the way back you go through the Papanikólaos Cave

of Meganísi, stop on the beach of the Onássis island of Skórpios for a swim before stopping at the small private island of Madoúri *(bookings at the harbour | 25 euros)*.

For a very romantic day you should take a cruise on the 'Odysseía'. The galleon is a replica of the mythological boat of Odysseus and was built in Vlichó on Léfkas. It departs daily from Nidrí on a cruise to Meganísi and Skórpios. On the way there is plenty of time for swimming, snorkelling and fishing. A barbeque is also included in the itinerary *(40 euros)*. Information at the harbour in Nidrí and in all the travel agencies on Léfkas. In ad-

From biking to windsurfing: the best places for your favourite sport and where you can also find out as much information in advance

dition, tours are offered several times a week around Léfkas, with swimming breaks on the beaches of Káthisma, Pórto Katsíki as well as Vassilikí *(25 euros)*. Information available in travel agencies and on the excursion boats themselves.

There are three to four pleasure boats on Zákynthos who offer trips around the island, their itineraries are all more or less identical. They include at least two swimming breaks, one of which is Ship-wreck Beach *(tickets at travel agencies on the coastal road | price from the harbour 25 euros)*.

COOKING COURSES

On Kefaloniá ● Vassilikí and Giórgos Balí offer the opportunity to INSIDER TIP cook Greek food with them three times a week.

Friday, fish and seafood are on the menu, Thursday and Saturday it is meat and vegetables. The fresh produce, such as herbs and salad leaves, are first gathered from their own garden and the culinary fruits of your labour are enjoyed together afterwards at a festive table. *Karavádos | tel. 26 71 06 94 53 | www.chezvassiliki.gr | 60 euros/person including wine and a recipe booklet*

CYCLING

Kefaloniá and Léfkas are ideal for ambitious mountain bikers; one can still find several tracks in the mountains that have, at the most, only been explored by a few Jeeps. On Kefaloniá you can get a good bike and tips at *Ideal Bikes (Odós Souidás 15 | Argostóli | tel. 26 71 02 80 74)*. They also rent out good child seats and even bicycle trailers. If there are still spots available, you can book day trips and tour packages on Léfkas at *Áthos Travel (Nidrí | on the main thoroughfare at the harbour | tel. 26 45 09 21 85)*. They also rent basic mountain bikes to individuals *(from 5 euros per day)*. On Zákynthos rental bikes and basic mountain bikes are available at all the holiday resorts.

DIVING

The ideal spot for divers is the ★ coast pitted with caves along the peninsula in the south-west of Límni Kerioú on Zákynthos. There are ● two very good dive centres with a lot of experience: *Turtle Beach Diving Centre, Timothéos Marmíris (Limní Kerioú | harbour | tel. 26 95 04 87 68 | www. diving-center-turtle-beach.com)* and the *Neró Sport Diving Center (Peter & Dennis Mohr | Límni Kerioú, west of the harbour | tel. 26 95 02 84 81)*.
A good dive school on Léfkas is the *Léfkas Diving Center* in Nikianá *(tel. 26 45 07 21 05 |* *www.lefkasdivingcenter.gr)*. Another diving centre is located on the beach in Vassilikí on Léfkas: *Diving Vassilikí | mobile tel. 69 39 34 13 32 | www.scuba-ski.com*.

HORSEBACK RIDING

For riding enthusiasts there are some INSIDER TIP excellent stables at Zerváta on Kefaloniá. Owner Cornelia Schimpfky stables the sure-footed Haflingers and offers rides – from several hours to multi-day – as well as lessons in jumping and dressage *(tel. 26 74 02 31 43, mobile tel. 69 77 53 32 03 | www.kephalonia.com/ English/Welcome.html)*.
On Zákynthos Nána Tsouráki has more than 50 ponies and horses for beginners and experienced riders alike. She is environmentally conscious and as such does not offer 😊 beach rides, only cross-country rides *(well signposted off the Argássi– Kalamáki road, | tel. 26 95 02 31 95, mobile tel. 69 44 52 05 19 | daily from 7am | free shuttle service to hotel | 1 hour 20 euros, 2 hours 35 euros)*.

HIKING

When hiking you should always wear long pants due to the thorny undergrowth and good footwear is also essential. There are no accurate hiking maps, a few marked trails only on Kefaloniá and Ithaca.

MOTOR BOATS

In Greece boats with engines up to 30 horsepower can be rented by adults even without a boating license. Daily fees depend on the power and the season, anywhere from 40–105 euros per day. Rentals include, for example, in Fiskárdo on Kefaloniá *(Fiscardo Boat Hire in the harbour | tel. 26 74 04 13 17 | www.fiscardo. com/rent_a_boat.htm)*, in Nidrí on Léfkas

All of the islands offer boat excursions to swimming bays, such as here on Zákynthos

(Avis | on the main thoroughfare | tel. 26 45 09 21 36) and in Alikés on Zákynthos *(Golden Dolfin | north of the beach area | tel. 26 95 08 32 48 | www.alykes.com).*

SAILING

Sailing opportunities are available from Nikianá on Léfkas and from Fiskárdo on Kefaloniá. The cruises take one or two weeks and even offer the beginner the opportunity to sail the area alone, as the experienced crew ensure safety from an accompanying boat. Organiser: *Sunsail* *(www.sunsail.co.uk). Skorpios-Charter (tel. 26 45 09 22 81 | www.skorpioscharter.com)* offer trips from Nidrí on Léfkas.

SEA KAYAKING

INSIDER TIP *Seakayaking Kefaloniá* offer a unique experience in Greece. The small company, run by the Swiss-Greek couple Yvonne and Pávlos, offer ten different day trips (each trip 60 euros) along the coast of Kefaloniá. Ideal for all ages and also for beginners. Also eight to nine day kayak tours to, among others, Léfkas, Meganísi, Kastós, Kálamos and Ithaca. *(Trapesáki | mobile tel. 69 34 01 04 00 | www.seakay-akingkefalonia-greece.com)*

WATER SPORTS

With the exception of Ithaca, there are water sport centres (usually right in front of the large hotels) on all of the islands, where you can rent pedal boats, go water-skiing and kitesurfing.

WINDSURFING

On Léfkas many beaches have windsurf-ing centres. Some of the good ones are *Club Vassiliki Active Holidays (on Vassilikí beach | tel. 26 45 03 15 88 | www.clubvass. com)* and the *Mílos Windsurf Club (in the very windy region of Ágios Ioánnis near Lefkáda | mobile tel. 69 73 75 83 76 | www. milosbeach.gr).*

TRAVEL WITH KIDS

Ithaca, Kefaloniá, Léfkas and Zákynthos are relatively small islands with relatively few permanent residents. That is why it is not viable to set up amusement parks, zoos and water parks for the locals.

There is absolutely no mass tourism on Ithaca and Kefaloniá, and on Léfkas it is still in its infancy. That is why no major investments of this kind have been made even for the tourists. There are a few modest developments on Zákynthos.

The lack of these kinds of facilities, which seem essential to us for a family holiday, lies in the fact that the Greeks are very child friendly – they let their children take part in almost everything that older persons do – until well after midnight. Children are welcome guests at night in café bars and tavernas; they can romp around in public places, between the locals out for a stroll and even play soccer in front of the church. With many of the sporting facilities and water activities there are no set age limits so whatever the children are able to do (and what their parents allow them to do) is available for them to try.

The good weather, wonderful beaches and sea all mean that children are seldom bored. All the islands (except Ithaca) have more than enough shallow, shel-

Photo: Coast between Skála and Póros on Kefaloniá

Lots of fun for children and parents: the best ideas for some adventures in the water, on the sea and on land

tered bays where little ones can splash and swim. Almost all of the large hotels on Zákynthos also have wading pools. Boat trips are always great adventures and if you are experienced enough, then you can even INSIDER TIP rent a motor boat and the children will love being sailors and cabin crew.

Walks here are fun even for children who are reluctant to walk with their parents

at home. On the Greek Islands there are no boring and crowded trails; instead the routes are mostly used by shepherds or goat paths. Along the way there are countless lizards and sometimes you can even spot snakes. There are seldom any 'do not' signs so the children can scramble around as and where as they wish – even in the ruins and medieval castles that are almost never secured!

overuse of antibiotics then it is best that you also pack your home remedies.

Child discounts are offered on public buses, on domestic flights, on ships and excursion boats as well as on many of the excursions for children under 12 years old. Visits to the state museums and archaeological sites are free of charge for children. Since there are no attractions specifically aimed at children on the other islands, the following recommendations are limited to Kefaloniá and Zákynthos.

KEFALONIÁ

PLAY CHAUFFEUR
(120 B2) (*◫ B12*)

When the sandman comes for children elsewhere, children in Greece may stay up and get behind the wheel of a Jeep or a VW Beetle. In good weather the small electric cars are available daily in Argostóli in the *Luna Park* fun fair at the northern end of Odós Rizospáston *(5 euros for 15 minutes)*. The park also has remote controlled boats, table soccer and other games.

MINIATURE TRAIN ON WHEELS
(120 B2) (*◫ B11–12*)

Miniature trains with locomotives and three wagons, with space for about 20 people, are popular throughout Greece. They are driven by electric motors and have rubber wheels. *Argostóli* has one that runs through the town. *Departure from the harbour, daily 8.30am–10.30pm | trip 3.50 euros, children 2 euros*

FUN & GAMES
(120 C3) (*◫ C12*)

In *Paidotopos Prókris* parents can enjoy their coffee in the adjoining café in a beautiful garden, while children jump on the trampolines, bowl or play basketball. Fifteen other games are available

Inquisitive goat in Áskos Stonepark

There are doctors who are familiar with all the usual childhood diseases, on all of the islands. Greek doctors prescribe antibiotics very readily, even for minor illnesses. So if you are critical about the

and there are also various events and activities such as childrens' theatre, crafts and dance lessons. Barbeques take place on weekends. *All year round | Mazarakáta, below the Ágios Geórgios fortress | Mon–Fri 6pm–10.30pm, Sat/Sun 11am–10.30pm | 4 euros per child flat rate for all games*

ZÁKYNTHOS

HORSE-DRAWN CARRIAGE RIDE ●
(123 E4) (*W F16–17*)

In the late afternoon horse-drawn carriages line the *Ágios Nikólaos pier* at the edge of the Platía Solomoú in Zákynthos Town. Trips through the island capital take 20 minute and if the little ones feel brave enough then they are often also allowed to hold the reins and may sit next to the driver. Carriages are also available in *Alikés, where they usually wait for customers on the road that runs parallel to the beach. 20 euros for 20 minute trips; in the off season you may be able to bargain the price down to 15 euros.*

PLAY CHAUFFEUR
(123 E4) (*W F16–17*)

On Zákynthos there are also small electric cars for children. In INSIDER TIP good weather daily from 6pm on the *Platía Solomoú* in Zákynthos Town, and they sometimes operate until well after 10pm. The only requirement: little ones should already be able to hold a steering wheel and to step on the pedal – which is often easier than taking their foot off the pedal. The cars have space for two children or one child and a parent (very lightweight) who wants to ride along. Parents need to keep an eye on their children as the area is not fenced. Runaways can drive anywhere from here – for as long as their batteries last. *4 euros for 15 minutes*

MINIATURE TRAIN ON WHEELS
(123 E4) (*W F16–17*)

Zákynthos has two miniature trains on wheels: one travels from Alikés to Pigadákia *(see p. 73)* and is also entertaining for adults while the second one goes between Argássi and the island capital. Departure in *Argássi* at the *Hotel Mimóza* on the main thoroughfare, in *Zákynthos Town* at *Platía Solomoú. Times depend on the season, but usually daily 10am–1pm and 5pm–10pm | trip 3.50 euros, children 2 euros*

ANIMALS UP CLOSE
(122 B2) (*W D15*)

The *Áskos Stonepark* is scenically situated between some hills in the north of the island. The park has sheep and goats, rabbits, tortoises, birds of prey and peacocks, lizards, donkeys and ponies, raccoons and many more animals. There are also ancient cisterns, cottages, stables as well as a stone wine press. The admission price is, however, disproportionate for this park, which is still under construction. *May–Sept daily 9am–7pm, Oct–April daily 10am–5pm | admission 8.50 euros, children (5–12 years) 5 euros | Áskos | www.askosstonepark.gr*

FUN WITHOUT THE PARENTS
(123 F5) (*W G17*)

On Zákynthos, more so than on the other islands, the large hotels provide entertainment during the day for children under 12 such as the all inclusive hotel *Eleon Grand Resort* in Traganáki *(tel. 26 95 06 52 45 | www.eleon-grand-resort.gr | Expensive)* and the all inclusive hotel *Louis Zante Beach* in Laganás *(tel. 26 95 05 11 30 | www.louishotel.com | Expensive)*. Both hotels are right on the beach and their services allow parents some time to themselves. Book the best package through your travel agent.

FESTIVALS & EVENTS

On the southern Ionian Islands many religious festivals are celebrated with traditional music, dancing and good food. Local communities and associations ensure that island culture is not neglected even during the summer. Festivals are not only organised for tourists, but also give the many Greek visitors a taste of the culture of the respective island.

The most important festival of the year is Easter. Like many other movable religious festivals, this date is set according to the Julian calendar. Easter can take place up to five weeks later than elsewhere.

PUBLIC HOLIDAYS

1 January *New Year;* **6 January** *Epiphany;* **Shrove Monday** *(3 March 2014, 23 February 2015, 14 March 2016)*; **25 March** *Independence;* **Good Friday**; **Easter** *(20/21 April 2014, 12/13 April 2015, 1/2 May 2016)*; **1 May** *Workers' Day;* **21 May** *Unification of the Ionian Islands;* **Pentecost** *(8/9 June 2014, 31 May/1 June 2015, 19/20 June 2016)*; **15 August** *Assumption Day;* **28 October** *National day;* **25/26 December** *Christmas*

FESTIVALS & EVENTS

FEBRUARY/MARCH
▶ *Carnival Sunday:* Carnival processions in all of the islands' capitals. The best one is the one in Zákynthos Town

APRIL–JUNE
▶ *Good Friday:* in the morning the symbolic grave of Christ is decorated with flowers in all the churches. Evening processions in all the towns and villages
▶ *Easter Saturday:* Easter mass from 11pm, which almost all Greeks attend. Shortly before midnight all the lights are turned off in the church. At midnight the priest announces the resurrection of Christ. The worshippers light candles and there are fireworks
▶ *Easter Sunday:* Lamb and kid on the spit, after lunch everyone celebrates with their family
▶ *Easter Monday:* Large church festival in Kerí on Zákynthos
▶ *Unification of the Ionian Islands:* on 21 May the unification with Greece is celebrated in all the capitals

The events calendar highlight is Easter: a whole series of religious celebrations and cultural festivals

▶ **Pentecost Monday:** church festival in Macherádo on Zákynthos

JULY–SEPTEMBER

▶ **Cultural summer** in Argostóli on Kefaloniá and in the villages in the region with theatre performances, concerts of all kinds and folk performances. *Early July–25 August*

▶ **Church festival** in Nidrí on Léfkas. *7 July*

▶ **Wine festival on a Sunday** in Ágios Ilías on Léfkas. *Second half of July*

▶ **Church festival** in Exógi in the north of Ithaca with music and dance. *17 July*

▶ **Church festival** in Kióni on Ithaca with music, dance and lamb on the spit. *20 July*

▶ *Church festival* in Pigadákia on Zákynthos. *27 July*

One evening in August in the mountain village Kariá on Léfkas a traditional ▶ INSIDER TIP **Lefkadian wedding** is recreated and then celebrated on the village square just like in the old days. *Early August*

Large ▶ **church festival** in Stavrós on Ithaca. *5/6 August*

The largest ▶ **church festival** of the summer is celebrated in many villages, such as in Vassilikí on Léfkas and in Lixoúri on Kefaloniá. *15 August*

Week-long ▶ **International Folklore Festival** on Léfkas with participants from more than twenty countries. *Second half of August*

The large ▶ **festival of Saint Dioníssios** in Zákynthos Town is attended by many Greeks from the mainland. From about 7pm ceremonial procession with fireworks, afterwards festival in the streets and in the tavernas. *24 August*

On the evening of 6 September ▶ **church service and festival** at the Monastery of Katharón on Ithaca, on the next morning ▶ **icon procession** with orchestral accompaniment. *6/7 September*

LINKS, BLOGS, APPS & MORE

LINKS

▶ odysseus.culture.gr/index_en.html official website of the Greek Ministry of Culture with lots of information and pictures of archaeological sites and museums, unfortunately not always up to date

▶ www.theionian.com online edition of monthly Ionian Islands magazine with current events, timetables for ferries and buses, reports and an annual photo contest

▶ www.ekathimerini.com daily English language newspaper that provides a comprehensive summary of the main political, business, social and cultural news in Greece

▶ www.visitgreece.gr/en/greek_ islands/ionian_islands/zakynthos a website with information on the island's history, culture and beaches.

▶ www.zanteweb.gr your destination at a glance: map, beaches, sightseeing, weather and a link to discussion forums

▶ www.bbc.co.uk/languages/greek for some essential Greek phrases and an introduction to basic Greek as well as links to other free courses, a slide show and video

BLOGS & FORUMS

▶ www.livinginzante.com a comprehensive site set up for expats wanting to live in Zákynthos, with lots of very useful links for tourists about the various services on the island

▶ www.travelblog.org/Europe/ Greece with about 200 blogs about Zákynthos and its neighbouring islands

Regardless of whether you are still preparing your trip or already on the Ionian Islands: these addresses will provide you with more information, videos and networks to make your holiday even more enjoyable

▶ www.greeka.com/ionian/kefalonia/kefalonia-videos-1.htm about 50 videos on different aspects of the island of Kefaloniá

▶ www.aroundgreece.com/ionian/ithaca/videos-ithaca.php collection of videos about Ithaca from different sources

▶ www.greeka.com/ionian/zakynthos/zakynthos-videos-1.htm a selection of about 20 videos in different languages on the island of Zákynthos

▶ iZante Travel Guide and iKefalonia are two free apps with general information on the islands of Zákynthos und Kefaloniá

▶ Ithacagreece.com is a mobile app for the island of Ithaca

▶ Marine Traffic is a popular online service (paid app) for vessel tracking. The vessel's name allows you to see where it comes from, where it is headed to and other data about the ship, the flag, etc. Also handy for tracking the local ferries

▶ Jourist World 'Travel Interpreter' is an inexpensive app that is tailored to the translation needs of tourists. The audio translations are helpful and entertaining and are accompanied by some funny illustrations

▶ www.facebook.com/pages/Greek-Islands/101480387302 the ideal online community, with lots of beautiful pictures and you can make your own images accessible to a worldwide audience

▶ www.virtualzakynthos.gr An innovative virtual tourist and business guide to Zákynthos created by using a panoramic photography technique. The guide covers the main tourist areas of the island

▶ www.airbnb.com/s/Zakynthos Airbnb is a popular site for travellers and there are numerous Zákynthos listings that range from a room in a private home through to a luxury villa with a private pool and magnificent sea views. The site is constantly updated with new listings and user reviews

TRAVEL TIPS

ARRIVAL

During the summer there are several flights to Zákynthos. Only a few chartered flights go to Préveza/Léfkas and to Kefaloniá. There are regular flights to Zákynthos, Kefaloniá and Léfkas all year round from Athens. Enough taxis are available at all airports, there are no airport buses. You can only get to Ithaca by boat, the best way is from Pátras or Kefaloniá. Flights in the turbo-props of the Cretan airline *Sky Express* (www.skyexpress.gr) are state-subsidised making them very affordable: Préveza to Kefaloniá (50 euros), to Zákynthos (55 euros), and between Kefaloniá and Zákynthos (55 euros). Because they fly at low altitudes, these flights are recommended for day trippers! Even Kíthira off the south coast of the Peloponnese (historically part of the Ionian Islands) and Corfu, the main island of the archipelago, are also accessible on from Zákynthos, Kefaloniá and Préveza.

Car ferries connect Igoumenítsa on the mainland (for Léfkas) and Pátras on the Peloponnese (for the remaining islands) throughout the year with the Italian ports of Ancona, Brindisi and Bari. A car ferry departs for Kefaloniá from Brindisi every third day in June, July and August. Info: Endeavor Lines | tel. 2109 40 52 22 | www.endeavorlines.com

BUSES

There are public buses on all the Ionian Islands. The fares are low and tickets are sold by the conductor in the bus. Timetable copies are available at the bus terminals of the respective islands. The timetables change several times a year depending on the season. The buses run less frequently on Saturdays and Sundays.

CAMPING

Camping anywhere else but in a camp site is prohibited but is often done on isolated beaches. Many of the islands have official campsites and they are open between May and September.

CAR HIRE

Bicycles, mopeds, motor scooters, motorbikes and cars are available for rent on most of the islands. To rent a car you must have had your driver's license for more than a year and be over 21. A small car will cost about 35 euros per day including mileage, full comprehensive cover and tax.

Caution: damage to the tyres and on the underside of the car is usually not covered by insurance.

RESPONSIBLE TRAVEL

It doesn't take a lot to be environmentally friendly whilst travelling. Don't just think about your carbon footprint whilst flying to and from your holiday destination but also about how you can protect nature and culture abroad. As a tourist it is especially important to respect nature, look out for local products, cycle instead of driving, save water and much more. If you would like to find out more about eco-tourism please visit: www.ecotourism.org

From arrival to weather

Holiday from start to finish: the most important addresses and information for your trip to the Ionian Islands

CONSULATES & EMBASSIES

UK EMBASSY
1 Ploutarchou Street | 10675 Athens | tel. 210 727 2600 | consular.athens@fco.gov.uk

UK CONSULATE
28 Foskolou Street | 29100 Zákynthos | tel. 26 95 02 2906| Zakynthos@fco.gov.uk

US EMBASSY
91 Vasilissis Sophias Avenue | Athens | tel. 210 721 2951 | AthensAmEmb@state.gov

CANADIAN EMBASSY
4 Ioannou Ghennadiou Street | 11521 Athens | tel. 210 727 3400 | www.canada international.gc.ca/greece-grece

CUSTOMS

For EU citizens the following duty free allowances apply (import and export): for own consumption 800 cigarettes, 400 cigarillos, 200 cigars, 1kg tobacco, 20L aperitif, 90L wine (with a maximum amount of 60L sparkling wine) and 110L beer.
Travellers to the US who are residents of the country do not have to pay duty on articles purchased overseas up to the value of $800, but there are limits on the amount of alcoholic beverages and tobacco products. For the regulations for international travel for US residents please see *www.cbp.gov*

DRINKING WATER

It is safe to drink the chlorinated tap water everywhere. Still mineral water *(metallikó neró)* is also available on ferries, in restaurants and cafés and is usually the same price as in the supermarkets.

CURRENCY CONVERTER

£	€	€	£
1	1.30	1	0.80
3	3.80	3	2.40
5	6.30	5	4
13	16.30	13	10
40	50	40	32
75	94	75	60
120	150	120	96
250	313	250	200
500	625	500	400

$	€	€	$
1	0.80	1	1.30
3	2.30	3	3.90
5	3.80	5	6.50
13	10	13	11
40	30.80	40	52
75	58	75	98
120	92	120	156
250	192	250	325
500	385	500	650

For current exchange rates see www.xe.com

DRIVING

For the entry with your own car, a national license and the motor vehicle registration should suffice; an international green insurance card is recommended. There is a good network of the petrol stations on the islands. The use of seatbelts is compulsory for drivers and front passengers. The maximum speed in the towns is 50km/30mi, on national roads 90km/56mi. Maximum blood alcohol limit is 0.5 and 0.1 for motorcycle riders.

Parking in a no parking zone is expensive: the fine costs 80 euros, most traffic violations are fined very heavily in Greece.

EARTHQUAKES

Light earthquakes do occur now and then and should you experience an earthquake take cover underneath a table or a bed. As soon as the quake is over you should go outside (do not use the lifts) and then stay clear of walls and flower pots that might fall over. Once outside follow the lead of the locals.

ELECTRICITY

Greece has the same 220 volt as most continental European countries. You will need an adapter if you want to use a UK plug.

EMERGENCY SERVICES

Dial *112* for all the emergency services: police, fire brigade and ambulance. The number is toll free and English is also spoken.

ENTRANCE FEES

From November to March, entrance is free on Sundays for all visitors. Other free entrance days are the first Sunday in April, May and October, the 6th of March, the last weekend in September, all international observances such as the International Remembrance Day in April, International Museum Day in May, World Environment Day in June and World Tourism Day in September. Admission to dance clubs is mostly free, but the drinks are usually more expensive.

FERRIES

Large car ferries travel between Sámi/Kefaloniá and Vathí/Ithaca, otherwise only small car ferries travel between the islands. From Ágios Nikólaos on Zákynthos in midsummer you can get to Pessáda on Kefaloniá. In summer ferries go from Fiskárdo or Agía Evfimía (on Kefaloniá) to Alalkoménes (on Ithaca) and from Fiskárdo and Fríkes to Vassilikí and Nidrí (on Léfkas).

HEALTH

Well-trained doctors guarantee basic medical care on all major islands, however there is often a lack of technical equipment. If you are seriously ill, it is advisable to return home and this will be covered by your travel insurance.

Emergency treatment in hospitals is free of charge and you can by treated for free by doctors if you present the European Health Insurance Card issued by your own insurance company. However, in practice this is complicated and doctors do so reluctantly and it is better to pay cash, get a receipt and then present your bills to the insurance company for a refund.

There are pharmacies in the larger towns and villages; on the smaller islands, doctors have medication on hand for emergencies.

IMMIGRATION

You will need a valid passport – even though it is no longer checked on immigration from Schengen countries – and should have it on you at all times in the case of police checks (for motorists), or when notifying a theft etc. Tourists from America, Canada and Australia do not need a visa for stays under 90 days.

INFORMATION

The Hellenic Ministry of Culture and Tourism website has explanations, photographs and information on opening times and entrance prices of all excavations and many museums: *www.culture.gr*

GREEK NATIONAL TOURISM ORGANISATION (UK)

4 Conduit Street | London, W1S 2DJ | tel. 020 7495 9300 | www.visitgreece.com

GREEK NATIONAL TOURISM ORGANISATION (USA)

305 East 47th Street, 2nd Floor | New York, NY 10017/tel. 212 421 5777 | www.greek tourism.com

INTERNET & WI-FI

Many hotels and cafés offer free Wi-Fi to guests with their own laptop, iPhone or Smartphone. Internet terminals are available in some travel agencies at a fee. Internet cafés are used primarily for computer games by young locals.

LANGUAGE

The Greeks are proud of the characters in their language which are unique to Greece. Although place names and labels are often also written in Roman letters, it is still useful to have some knowledge of the Greek alphabet – and you really need to know how to stress the words correctly to be understood. The vowel with the accent is emphasised. The transcription of Greek names in the map section of this guide is based on the recommended international UN style. However, as this is seldom used on the islands, the text section of this guidebook is orientated on the standard pronunciation and

spelling style used locally. The same place name and its surroundings can have up to four different versions.

MONEY & PRICES

The national currency is the euro and you can withdraw money from many ATMs with your credit or debit card. Often your own bank will charge a fee, depending on the amount, sometimes making it cheaper to draw a large amount at once instead of a lot of small amounts. Traveller's cheques are cashed at all banks and post offices. *Opening hours of the banks Mon–Thu 8am–2pm, Fri 8am–1.30pm.*

BUDGETING

Coffee	£2/$3.50	*for a cup of mocha*
Taxi	£0.60/$0.95	*per kilometre*
Wine	£2/$3.50	*for a glass of table wine*
Gyros	£2/$3.50	*for a portion in pita bread*
Petrol	£1.50/$2.50	*for 1 liter super*
Deck chair	£3.50–£7/$5.50–£11	*for two with umbrella*

Price levels are more or less the same as elsewhere in Europe. Hotel rooms and public transport are cheaper, petrol and foodstuff more expensive.

NEWSPAPERS

English magazines and newspapers are available at most holiday resorts on the island within a day or two of publication.

The weekly English *Athens News* is also published.

NUDIST BEACHES

Nude bathing is prohibited, but is practised on some of the isolated beaches. Topless sunbathing is accepted everywhere.

OPENING HOURS

Shops for the tourist trade are open daily 10am–10pm. Supermarkets are usually open from Monday to Saturday 8am–8pm. Many non-tourist shops are closed on Monday and Wednesday afternoons. The majority of restaurants are open daily in high season; dance clubs usually only open at about 11pm or midnight. The opening hours specified in this travel guide are subject to frequent changes.

PHONE & MOBILE PHONE

With the exception of some emergency numbers, all Greek telephone numbers have ten digits. There is no area dialling code. Greek mobile phone numbers always begin with '6'. Telephone booths with card telephones are very common in the towns, villages and on country roads. They are mainly operated by the telephone company OTE/COSMOTE which has of-

WEATHER ON ZÁKYNTHOS

	Jan	Feb	March	April	May	June	July	Aug	Sept	Oct	Nov	Dec
Daytime temperatures in °C/°F												
	14/57	14/57	16/61	19/66	24/75	28/82	31/88	32/90	28/82	23/73	19/66	16/61
Nighttime temperatures in °C/°F												
	5/41	5/41	7/45	9/48	12/54	16/61	18/64	18/64	16/61	13/55	10/50	7/45
Sunshine hours/day												
	4	5	6	8	10	10	13	11	9	7	5	3
Precipitation days/month												
	13	11	9	7	5	2	1	1	5	9	12	15
Water temperatures in °C/°F												
	14/57	14/57	14/57	16/61	18/64	21/70	23/73	24/75	23/73	21/70	18/64	16/61

fices in most cities. Telephone cards can be bought at kiosks and supermarkets. Mobile phones are popular in Greece and the reception is good. When buying a Greek SIM card to obtain a Greek number, you will always have to present identification. SIM cards can be bought from 5 euros and are valid for a year after the last use. Mobile service providers are Cosmote, Vodafone and Wind.

The dialling code for Greece is *+30* followed by the full ten digit telephone number. International dialling codes: UK *+44*, Australia *+61*, Canada *+1*, Ireland *+353*, and USA *+1*.

POST

There are post offices in all the towns and on almost all islands; they are mostly open from Monday to Friday 7am–3pm.

SMOKING

Smoking is prohibited in all enclosed public areas. However, outside of the towns and tourist centres the regulation is not taken seriously. The prices of cigarettes are slightly cheaper than elsewhere in Europe, and tobacco and cigarette paper is also available if you roll your own cigarettes.

TAXI

Taxis are plentiful on all the islands. Only in the larger cities like Zákynthos Town are they equipped with taxi meters. In all the other cases the taxi (called *agoréon*) driver calculates the price according to the distance.

TIME

Greece is two hours ahead of Greenwich Mean Time, seven hours ahead of US Eastern Time and seven hours behind Australian Eastern Time.

TIPPING

10–15 per cent; tips below 50 cents are insulting. Chambermaids get 1 euro per room per day; in taxis you can round up the fare.

TOILETS

Apart from those in the hotels, Greek toilets my hold some surprises. Sometimes they are smart and fitted with modern Italian plumbing; others should be used only in emergencies. Even in good hotels, you are not allowed to flush the used toilet paper, but you have to put it in the bin provided. The reason for this is that it clogs up the narrow sewers and soakaways.

TOURS

Excursions by boat or bus are on offer in the larger holiday resorts and hotels, especially on Zákynthos. Bus tours normally take place with a local, government-licensed tour guide. The boat excursions on Zákynthos may also include a bus transfer from the hotel to the harbour and back.

WHEN TO GO

The Ionian Islands are suitable only in the summer months as a tourist destination. Since almost all of them depend very much on tourism, many shops, restaurants, and hotels are closed from mid-October until April. During this time the islands can seem eerily empty, transport links are limited and the weather can also be very unpleasant due to storms and rainfall.

USEFUL PHRASES GREEK

PRONUNCIATION

We have provided a simple pronunciation aid for the Greek words
(see middle column). Note the following:

'   the following syllable is emphasised

ð   in Greek (shown as "dh" in middle column) is like "th" in "there"

θ   in Greek (shown as "th" in middle column) is like "th" in "think"

X   in Greek (shown as "ch" in middle column) is like a rough "h" or
     "ch" in Scottish "loch"

Α α a	Η η i	Ν ν n	Τ τ t
Β β v	Θ θ th	Ξ ξ ks, x	Υ υ i, y
Γ γ g, y	Ι ι i, y	Ο ο o	Φ φ f
Δ δ th	Κ κ k	Π π p	Χ χ ch
Ε ε e	Λ λ l	Ρ ρ r	Ψ ψ ps
Ζ ζ z	Μ μ m	Σ σ, ς s, ss	Ω ώ o

IN BRIEF

Yes/No/Maybe	ne/'ochi/'issos	Ναι/Όχι/Ισως
Please/Thank you	paraka'lo/efcharis'to	Παρακαλώ/Ευχαριστώ
Sorry	sig'nomi	Συγνώμη
Excuse me	me sig'chorite	Με συγχωρείτε
May I ...?	epi'treppete ...?	Επιτρέπεται ...?
Pardon?	o'riste?	Ορίστε?
I would like to .../	'thelo .../	Θέλω .../
have you got ...?	'echete ...?	Έχετε ...?
How much is ...?	'posso 'kani ...?	Πόσο κάνει ...?
I (don't) like this	Af'to (dhen) mu a'ressi	Αυτό (δεν) μου αρέσει
good/bad	ka'llo/kak'ko	καλό/κακό
too much/much/little	'para pol'li/pol'li/'ligo	πάρα πολύ/πολύ/λίγο
everything/nothing	ólla/'tipottal	όλα/τίποτα
Help!/Attention!/	vo'ithia!/prosso'chi!/	Βοήθεια!/Προσοχή!/
Caution!	prosso'chi!	Προσοχή!
ambulance	astheno'forro	Ασθενοφόρο
police/	astino'mia/	Αστυνομία/
fire brigade	pirosvesti'ki	Πυροσβεστική
ban/	apa'gorefsi/	Απαγόρευση/
forbidden	apago'revete	απαγορεύεται
danger/dangerous	'kindinoss/epi'kindinoss	Κίνδυνος/επικίνδυνος

Milás elliniká?

"Do you speak Greek?" This guide will help you to say the basic words and phrases in Greek

GREETINGS, FAREWELL

Good morning!/afternoon!/evening!/night!	kalli'mera/kalli'mera!/kalli'spera!/kalli'nichta!	Καλημέρα/Καλημέρα!/Καλησπέρα!/Καληνύχτα!
Hello!/goodbye!	'ya (su/sass)!/a'dio!/ya (su/sass)!	Γεία (σου/σας)!/αντίο!/Γεία (σου/σας)!
Bye!	me 'lene ...	Με λένε …
My name is ...	poss sass 'lene?	Πως σας λένε?

DATE & TIME

Monday/Tuesday	dhef'tera/'triti	Δευτέρα/Τρίτη
Wednesday/Thursday	tet'tarti/'pempti	Τετάρτη/Πέμπτη
Friday/Saturday	paraske'vi/'savatto	Παρασκευή/Σάββατο
Sunday/weekday	kiria'ki/er'gassimi	Κυριακή/Εργάσιμη
today/tomorrow/yesterday	'simera/'avrio/chtess	Σήμερα/Αύριο/Χτες
What time is it?	ti 'ora 'ine?	Τι ώρα είναι?

TRAVEL

open/closed	annik'ta/klis'to	Ανοικτό/Κλειστό
entrance/driveway	'issodhos/'issodhos ochi'matonn	Είσοδος/Είσοδος οχημάτων
exit	'eksodhos/'Eksodos ochi'matonn	Έξοδος/Έξοδος οχημάτων
departure/departure/arrival	anna'chorissi/anna'chorissi/'afiksi	Αναχώρηση/Αναχώρηση/Άφιξη
toilets/restrooms / ladies/gentlemen	tual'lettes/gine'konn/an'dronn	Τουαλέτες/Γυναικών/Ανδρών
(no) drinking water	'possimo ne'ro	Πόσιμο νερό
Where is ...?/Where are ...?	pu 'ine ...?/pu 'ine ...?	Πού είναι/Πού είναι …?
bus/taxi	leofo'rio/tak'si	Λεωφορείο/Ταξί
street map/map	'chartis tis 'pollis/'chartis	Χάρτης της πόλης/Χάρτης
harbour	li'mani	Λιμάνι
airport	a-ero'drommio	Αεροδρόμιο
schedule/ticket	drommo'logio/issi'tirio	Δρομολόγιο/Εισιτήριο
I would like to rent ...	'thelo na nik'yasso ...	Θέλω να νοικιάσω …
a car/a bicycle/a boat	'enna afto'kinito/'enna po'dhilato/'mia 'varka	ένα αυτοκίνητο/ένα ποδήλατο/μία βάρκα
petrol/gas station	venzi'nadiko	Βενζινάδικο
petrol/gas / diesel	ven'zini/'diesel	Βενζίνη/Ντίζελ

FOOD & DRINK

Could you please book a table for tonight for four?	Klis'te mass parakal'lo 'enna tra'pezi ya a'popse ya 'tessera 'atoma	Κλείστε μας παρακαλώ ένα τραπέζι γιά απόψε γιά τέσσερα άτομα
The menu, please	tonn ka'taloggo parakal'lo	Τον κατάλογο παρακαλώ
Could I please have ...?	tha 'ithella na 'echo ...?	Θα ήθελα να έχω …?
with/without ice/ sparkling	me/cho'ris 'pago/ anthrakik'ko	με/χωρίς πάγο/ ανθρακικό
vegetarian/allergy	chorto'fagos/allerg'ia	Χορτοφάγος/Αλλεργία
May I have the bill, please?	'thel'lo na pli'rosso parakal'lo	Θέλω να πληρώσω παρακαλώ

SHOPPING

Where can I find...?	pu tha vro ...?	Που θα βρω …?
pharmacy/ chemist	farma'kio/ ka'tastima	Φαρμακείο/Κατάστημα καλλυντικών
bakery/market	'furnos/ago'ra	Φούρνος/Αγορά
grocery	pandopo'lio	Παντοπωλείο
kiosk	pe'riptero	Περίπτερο
expensive/cheap/price	akri'vos/fti'nos/ti'mi	ακριβός/φτηνός/Τιμή
more/less	pio/li'gotere	πιό/λιγότερο

ACCOMMODATION

I have booked a room	'kratissa 'enna do'matio	Κράτησα ένα δωμάτιο
Do you have any ... left?	'echete a'komma ...	Έχετε ακόμα …
single room	mon'noklino	Μονόκλινο
double room	'diklino	Δίκλινο
key	kli'dhi	Κλειδί
room card	ilektronni'ko kli'dhi	Ηλεκτρονικό κλειδί

HEALTH

doctor/dentist/ paediatrician	ya'tros/odhondoya'tros/ pe'dhiatros	Ιατρός/Οδοντογιατρός/ Παιδίατρος
hospital/ emergency clinic	nossoko'mio/ yatri'ko 'kentro	Νοσοκομείο/ Ιατρικό κέντρο
fever/pain	piret'tos/'ponnos	Πυρετός/Πόνος
diarrhoea/nausea	dhi'arria/ana'gula	Διάρροια/Αναγούλα
sunburn	ilia'ko 'engavma	Ηλιακό έγκαυμα
inflamed/ injured	molli'menno/ pligo'menno	μολυμένο /πληγωμένο
pain reliever/tablet	paf'siponna/'chapi	Παυσίπονο/Χάπι

POST, TELECOMMUNICATIONS & MEDIA

stamp/letter	gramma'tossimo/'gramma	Γραμματόσημο/Γράμμα
postcard	kartpos'tall	Καρτ-ποστάλ
I need a landline phone card	kri'azomme 'mia tile'karta ya dhi'mossio tilefoni'ko 'thalamo	Χρειάζομαι μία τηλεκάρτα για δημόσιο τηλεφωνικό θάλαμο
I'm looking for a prepaid card for my mobile	tha 'ithella 'mia 'karta ya to kinni'to mu	Θα ήθελα μία κάρτα για το κινητό μου
Where can I find internet access?	pu bor'ro na vro 'prosvassi sto índernett?	Που μπορώ να βρω πρόσβαση στο ίντερνετ?
socket/adapter/charger	'briza/an'dapporras/fortis'tis	πρίζα/αντάπτορας/φορτιστής
computer/battery/rechargeable battery	ippologis'tis/batta'ria/eppanaforti'zomenni batta'ria	Υπολογιστής/μπαταρία/επαναφορτιζόμενη μπαταρία
internet connection/wifi	'sindhessi se as'sirmato 'dhitio/vaifai	Σύνδεση σε ασύρματο δίκτυο/WiFi

LEISURE, SPORTS & BEACH

beach	para'lia	Παραλία
sunshade/lounger	om'brella/ksap'plostra	Ομπρέλα/Ξαπλώστρα

NUMBERS

0	mi'dhen	μηδέν
1	'enna	ένα
2	'dhio	δύο
3	'tria	τρία
4	'tessera	τέσσερα
5	'pende	πέντε
6	'eksi	έξι
7	ef'ta	εφτά
8	och'to	οχτώ
9	e'nea	εννέα
10	'dhekka	δέκα
11	'endhekka	ένδεκα
12	'dodhekka	δώδεκα
20	'ikossi	είκοσι
50	pen'inda	πενήντα
100	eka'to	εκατό
200	dhia'kossia	διακόσια
1000	'chilia	χίλια
10000	'dhekka chil'iades	δέκα χιλιάδες

NOTES

MARCO POLO TRAVEL GUIDES

- PACKED WITH INSIDER TIPS
- BEST WALKS AND TOURS
- FULL-COLOUR PULL-OUT MAP
  AND STREET ATLAS

ROAD ATLAS

The green line ____ indicates the Trips & Tours (p. 84–89)
The blue line ____ indicates The perfect route (p. 30–31)

All tours are also marked on the pull-out map

Photo: Zákynthos Town with harbour

Exploring the Ionian Islands

The map on the back cover shows how the area has been sub-divided

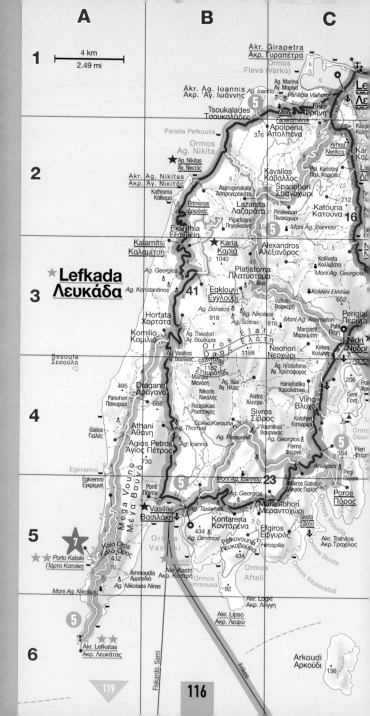

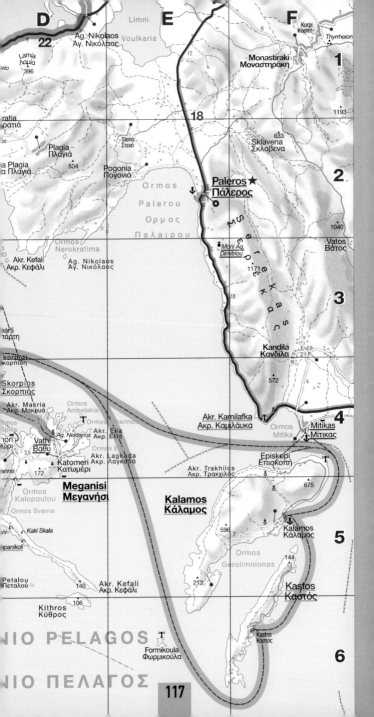

D 22

Limni

E

F

Ag. Nikolaos
Άγ. Νικόλαος

Voulkaria

Korpi
Κόρπη

Thyrrheion

Lamía
Λαμία
396

rio

Monastiraki
Μοναστηράκι

1

1193

ratia
ρατιά

Sklavena
Σκλάβενα

633

Plagia
Πλαγιά

Steno
Στενό

504

Pogonia
Πογονιά

Ormos
Palerou
Ορμος
Παλαιρού

Paleros ★
Πάλερος

2

1040

Vatos
Βάτος

Ormos
Nerokratima

Akr. Kefali
Ακρ. Κεφάλι

Ag. Nikolaos
Άγ. Νικόλαος

Mani Ag.
Dimitriou

1171

18

3

Kandila
Κανδήλα

572

arti
άρτη

Skorpios
Σκορπιός

Akr. Makria
Ακρ. Μακρυά

Ormos
Ambelakia

Akr. Kamilafka
Ακρ. Καμιλάυκα

Ormos
Mitika

Mitikas
Μίτικας

4

Spilia

Ag. Nektarios

Akr. Elia
Ακρ. Ελιά

Episkopi
Επισκοπή

Vathi
Βαθύ

Ormos E

Akr. Lagkada
Ακρ. Λαγκάδα

Katomeri
Κατωμέρι

172

Meganisi
Μεγανήσι

Kalamos
Κάλαμος

675

annis

Ormos
Kalopoulou

Ormos Svarna

Kaki Skala

596

Kalamos
Κάλαμος

5

Ormos
Gerolimnionas

144

Petalou
Πεταλού

Akr. Kefali
Ακρ. Κεφάλι

140

213

Kastos
Καστός

Kithros
Κύθρος

106

ΝΙΟ PELAGOS

Formikoula
Φωρμικούλα

Kastos
Καστός

6

ΝΙΟ ΠΕΛΑΓΟΣ

117

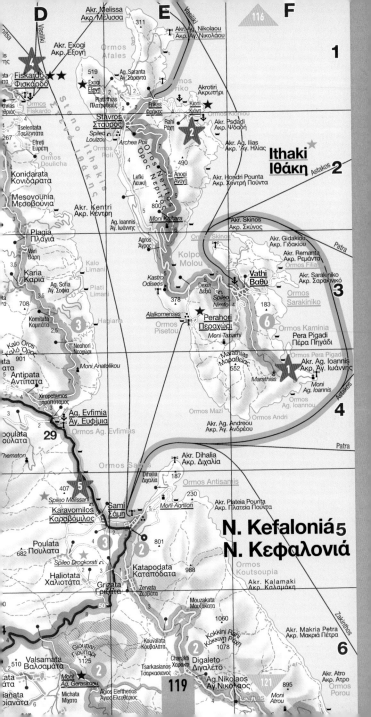

D

E

F

Akr. Melissa
Ακρ. Μέλισσα

311

1

Akr. Ag. Nikolaou
Ακρ. Αγ. Νικολάου

Akr. Exogi
Ακρ. Εξωγή

Ormos
Afales
Όρμος
Αφάλες

Akrotiri
Ακρωτήρι

Fiskardo
Φισκάρδο

519

Ag. Saranta
Αγ. Σαράντα

Ormos
Fiskardo
Όρμος
Φισκάρδο

Exogi
Εξωγή

Frikes
Φρίκες

Kioni
Κιόνι

thrias
θριάς

Platrithias
Πλατρίθειας

Stavros
Σταύρος

Akr. Psdadi
Ακρ. Ψδαδή

Tselentata
Τσελεντάτα

2

Rahi
Ράχη

267

Spileo
Louiza
Σπήλεο
Λουϊζα

Efreti
Ευρετή

Archea Poli
Αρχαία Πόλη

Akr. Ag. Ilias
Ακρ. Αγ. Ηλίας

Ormos
Doulicha
Όρμος
Δούλιχα

Ormos
Poli
Όρμος
Πόλη

Ithaki
Ιθάκη

Astakos

2

Konidarata
Κονιδάρατα

490

Anogi
Ανωγή

Akr. Hondri Pounta
Ακρ. Χόντρη Πούντα

Mesovounia
Μεσοβούνια

Lefki
Λευκή

Akr. Kentri
Ακρ. Κέντρι

800

Akr. Skinos
Ακρ. Σκίνος

Plagia
Πλαγιά

Vari
Βάρη

Ag. Ioannis
Αγ. Ιωάννης

Moni Kathara

Ormos Skinos

Akr. Gidakiou
Ακρ. Γιδακίου

Patra

Karia
Καριά

3.5

Ag. Sofia
Αγ. Σοφία

Agros
Άγρος

Kolpos
Molou

Akr. Remanta
Ακρ. Ρεμάντα

708

Plati
Limani

Ormos Filias

3.5

Kalo
Limani

Vathi
Βαθύ

Akr. Sarakiniko
Ακρ. Σαρακίνικο

Komitata
Κομιτάτα

Hagiana

Kastro
Odiseos

Dexia
Δεξιά

Ormos
Sarakiniko

2.5

3

378

Spileo
Nimfo

183

6

Kalo Oros
Καλό Όρος

901

Neohori
Νεοχώρι

Alalkomenses

Perahori
Περαχώρι

Ormos Kaminia

Antipata
Αντίπατα

Moni Anatolikou

Ormos
Pisetou

Moni Taxiarhi

Pera Pigadi
Πέρα Πηγάδι

Ormos Pera Pigadi

Xiropotamos
Ξηροπόταμος

Marathias
Μαραθείας
552

Akr. Ag. Ioannis
Ακρ. Αγ. Ιωάννης

1

Ag. Evfimia
Αγ. Ευφημία

Marathias

Moni
Ag. Ioannis

oulata
ούλατα

Ormos Ag. Evfimias

Ormos
Ag. Ioannou

29

Ormos Mazi

Astakos

4

hematon

Ormos Sames

Akr. Ag. Andreou
Ακρ. Αγ. Ανδρέου

Ormos Andri

Patra

Akr. Dihalia
Ακρ. Διχαλία

407

Dihalia
Διχαλία

187

Spileo Melissani

Ormos Antisamis

5

Karavomilos
Καραβόμιλος

Sami
Σάμη

230

Akr. Plateia Pounta
Ακρ. Πλατεία Πούντα

Moni Agrilion

Poulata
Πούλατα

682

3

801

N. Kefaloniá
Ν. Κεφαλονιά

5

Spileo Drogkorati

Katapodata
Καταπόδατα

988

Ormos
Koutsoupia

Haliotata
Χαλιωτάτα

Grizata
Γριζάτα

Zervata
Ζερβάτα

Akr. Kalamaki
Ακρ. Καλαμάκι

50

Mouzakata
Μουζακάτα

1060

Akr. Makria Petra
Ακρ. Μακριά Πέτρα

Valsamata
Βαλσαμάτα

510

Giourani
Γιουράνι
1125

Kouvalata
Κουβαλάτα

Kokkini Rahi
Κόκκινη Ράχη
1078

6

ata

2

Moni
Ag. Gerasimou

Tsarskasianos
Τσαρσκασιανός

Charakti
Χαρακτή

Digaleto
Διγαλέτο

Ag. Nikolaos
Αγ. Νίκολαος

2

Akr. Atro
Ακρ. Άτρο

895

Ormos
Porou

ianata

Michata
Μίχατα

Agios Eleftherios
Άγιος Ελευθέριος

121

Moni
Atrou

N. Kefaloniá
N. Κεφαλονιά[1]

eo Melissani
anomilos
ραβόμιλος

Moni Agnilion
230

801

Ormos
Koutsoupia

Akr. Kalamaki
Akr. Καλαμάκη

Spileo Drogkorati
iota
οτά

Katapodata
Καταπόδατα

988

Mouzakata
Μουζάκατα

Grizata
Γρίζατα

Zervata
Ζέρβατα

50

Akr. Makria Petra
Akr. Μακριά Πέτρα

1060

Giourari
Γιουράρι
1125

Kouvalata
Κουβάλατα

Kokkini Rahi
Κόκκινη Ράχη
1078

Digaleto
Διγαλέτο

Moni
Ag. Gerasimou

Tsarkasianos
Τσαρκασιάνος

Agios Nikolaos
Άγιος Νικόλαος

Akr. Atro
Akr. Άτρο

2

Michata
Μίχατα

Agios Eleftherios
Άγιος Ελευθέριος

Charakti
Χαράκτη

Avythos

Moni
Atrou

895

Ormos Porou
Poros
Πόρος

Epanohori
Επανοχώρι

1312

Akr. Pronnou
Akr. Πρόννου

Killini

Andriolata
Ανδριολάτα

268

Tzanata
Τζάνατα

403

Ormos
Gonies

Vlahata
Βλαχάτα

Enos
Ένος
1628

Xenopoulo
Ξενόπουλο

Agia Irini
Αγία Ειρήνη

Akr. Cheroulaki
Akr. Χερουλάκι

3

Mousata
ουσάτα

Simotata
Σιμωτάτα

Kapandriti
Καπανδρίτη

Annitata
Αννήτατα

Akr. Kapri
Akr. Κάπρι

Lourdata
Λουρδάτα

Kornelios
Κορνέλλος

Asprogerakas
Ασπρογέρακας

Ormos Lourda

Moni Sision

Arginia
Αργίνια

Ag. Georgios
Άγ. Γεώργιος

Pastra
Πάστρα

Spathi
Σπαθή

14

Platies
Πλατιές

Atsoupades
Ατσουπάδες

Koletis
Κολέτης

Proni

Valeriano
Βαλεριάνο

Hionata
Χιονάτα

Kremidi
Κρεμύδι

Faries
Φανιές

Thiramonas
θυραμονάς

Markopoulo
Μαρκόπουλο

Almata
Αλίματα

Skala
Σκάλα

Akr. Koronis
Akr. Κορώνης

Mavrata
Μαυράτα

Ratzakli
Ρατζάκλι

4

Akr. Apalohera
Akr. Απαλοχέρα

Akr. Katelios
Akr. Κατελιός

Kato Katelios
Κάτω Κατελιός

Ormos
Kateliou

Akr. Mounta
Akr. Μούντα

L A G O S

Killini

5

Ε Λ Α Γ Ο Σ

Ag. Nikolaos

6

N. Zakinthos
N. Ζάκινθος

Akr. Skinari
Akr. Σκινάρι

Korithi
Κόριθη

121

Galazio Spileo

122

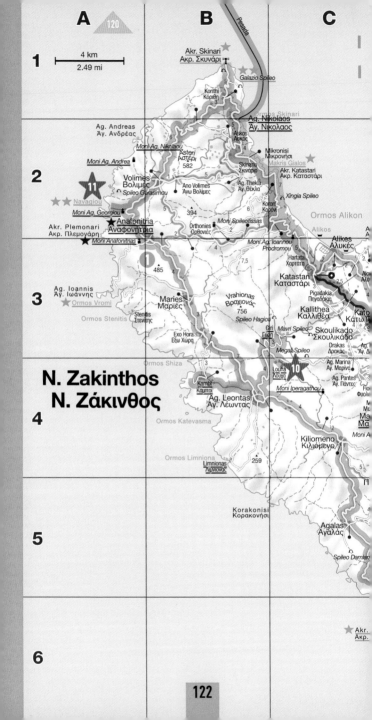

1

4 km
2.49 mi

Akr. Skinari
Ακρ. Σκυνάρι

Galazio Spileo

Korithi
Κόριθη

Aramba Skinari

Ag. Nikolaos
Άγ. Νικολαος

Ag. Andreas
Άγ. Ανδρέας

Askos
Ασκος

Moni Ag. Nikolaou

Asteri
Αστέρι
582

Mikronisi
Μικρονήσι

Makris Gialos

Moni Ag. Andrea

Skinario
Σκινάριο

Akr. Katastari
Ακρ. Καταστάρι

2

Volimes
Βολιμές

Ano Volimes
Ανω Βολιμές

Ag. Thekla
Αγ. θεκλα

7

11

Spileo Gerasimou

Xingia Spileo

Navagiou

394

Kotoni
Κοτονι

Moni Ag. Georgiou

Ormos Alikon

Akr. Plemonari
Ακρ. Πλεμονάρι

Anatonitria
Αναφονήτρια

Orthonies
Ορθονιές

Moni Spileotissas

Alikos

Alikes
Αλυκές

Moni Anafonitrias

Moni Ag. Ioannou
Prodromou

Aloi
Αλυ

485

Hartata
Χαρτάτα

7,5

Ag. Ioannis
Άγ. Ιωάννης

Katastari
Καταστάρι

2.5

Alo
Αλυ

Ormos Vromi

Pigadakia
Πηγαδάκια

3

Maries
Μαριές

Vrahionas
Βραχιονας
756

Kallithea
Καλλιθέα

Kato
Κάτω Π

Ormos Stenitis

Stenitis
Στενίτης

Spileo Hagioti

Skoulikado
Σκουλικάδο

Ag.
Άγ. Δ

Exo Hora
Εξω Χώρα

Giri
Γύρη

Mavri Spileo

Drakas
Δράκας

Megali Spileo

Ormos Shiza

Louha
Λούχα

10

Ag. Marina
Αγ. Μαρίνα

N. Zakinthos
N. Ζάκινθος

Kambi
Καμπί

Ag. Leontas
Άγ. Λέοντας

Moni Iperagathou

Ag. Pantes
Άγ. Πάντες

Fio
Φυσι

4

Ma
Μα

Ormos Katevasma

Moni A

Kiliomeno
Κιλιόμενο

Ormos Limniona

Limnionas
Λιμνιώνας

259

Korakonisi
Κορακονήσι

Agalas
Αγαλάς

5

Spileo Damian

Akr.
Ακρ.

6

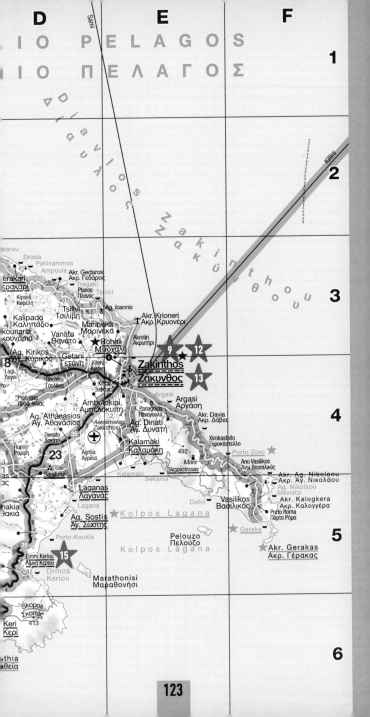

D　　　　E　　　　　　　　F

IO PELAGOS
IO ΠΕΛΑΓΟΣ

1

Adriavios Zakúnthou

Samí

2

Kilíni

3

sarou
Drosia
Pahinammos
Ampoula *Akr. Gedaros*
Planos *Akr. Γέδαρος*
erakari Tragaki
ερακαρi Πλάνος Tsilivi
Kipseli
Κιψέλη
Kalipado Tsilivi *Ag. Ioannis*
Καληπάδο Τσιλίβι
Marineka *Akr. Krioneri*
kounaria Vanato Μαρινέκα *Akr. Κρυονέρι*
κουνάρια Βανάτο ★Bohali *Akrotiri*
Ag. Kirikos Μπόχαλη *Akrotiri*
Αγ. Κύρικος Getani *Ak/ωτίρι*
Λαγι Getani Kiloni ★9 ★12
Λαγό Γετάνι Κιλώνι **Zakinthos**
Goulека Kifras **Ζάκυνθος** ★13
Προφ. Ηλίας Γουλέκα Σιφράς
Prof. Ilias Ambelokipi Argasi
Προφ. Ηλίας Αμπελόκιπη Panagoula Argasi Αργάση
Ag. Athanasios Παναγούλα *Akr. Davia*
Romiri Αγ. Αθανάσιος *Aerolimenas* *Akr. Δαβία*
Ρωμίρι *Zakinthou*
23 Ag. Dinati *Xirokastello*
Donato Αγ. Δυνατή Προκαστέλλο
Δώνατο Agrilia *Porto Zoro* ★
as Αγριλία Kalamaki 492 *Ano Vasilikos* ★ 4
ας *Sarakina* Καλαμάκι Μοni Άνω Βασιλικός
Skopiotissas *Akr. Ag. Nikolaou*
Kalamaki *Akr. Αγ. Νικολάου*
hakia Laganas *Ag. Nikolaou*
ακiά Λαγανάς *Sekania* *Mavratzi*
Lagana *Dafni* Vasilikos *Akr. Kalogkera*
Ag. Sostis Βασιλικός *Akr. Καλογγέρα*
Αγ. Σώστης *Kolpos Lagana* *Porto Roma*
Porto-Koukla Πόρτο Ρόμα
Geraka ★ 5
Limni Keriou ★15 *Kolpos Lagana* *Akr. Gerakas*
Αλμύρη Κεριού Pelouzo *Akr. Γέρακας*
Ormos Πελούζο
Keriou
Keri Marathonisi
Κεrί Μαραθονήσι
Skoros
Σκοπός
413
thia
θεία

6

KEY TO ROAD ATLAS

Motorway · Toll junction · Toll station · Junction with number · Motel · Restaurant · Snackbar · Filling-station · Parking place with and without WC	Autobahn · Gebührenpflichtige Anschlussstelle · Gebührenstelle · Anschlussstelle mit Nummer · Rasthaus mit Übernachtung · Raststätte · Kleinraststätte · Tankstelle · Parkplatz mit und ohne WC
Motorway under construction and projected with completion date	Autobahn in Bau und geplant mit Datum der Verkehrsübergabe
Dual carriageway (4 lanes)	Zweibahnige Straße (4-spurig)
Trunk road · Road numbers	Fernverkehrsstraße · Straßennummern
Important main road	Wichtige Hauptstraße
Main road · Tunnel · Bridge	Hauptstraße · Tunnel · Brücke
Minor roads	Nebenstraßen
Track · Footpath	Fahrweg · Fußweg
Tourist footpath (selection)	Wanderweg (Auswahl)
Main line railway	Eisenbahn mit Fernverkehr
Rack-railway, funicular	Zahnradbahn, Standseilbahn
Aerial cableway · Chair-lift	Kabinenschwebebahn · Sessellift
Car ferry · Passenger ferry	Autofähre · Personenfähre
Shipping route	Schifffahrtslinie
Nature reserve · Prohibited area	Naturschutzgebiet · Sperrgebiet
National park · natural park · Forest	Nationalpark · Naturpark · Wald
Road closed to motor vehicles	Straße für Kfz. gesperrt
Toll road	Straße mit Gebühr
Road closed in winter	Straße mit Wintersperre
Road closed or not recommended for caravans	Straße für Wohnanhänger gesperrt bzw. nicht empfehlenswert
Tourist route · Pass	Touristenstraße · Pass
Scenic view · Panoramic view · Route with beautiful scenery	Schöner Ausblick · Rundblick · Landschaftlich bes. schöne Strecke
Spa · Swimming pool	Heilbad · Schwimmbad
Youth hostel · Camping site	Jugendherberge · Campingplatz
Golf-course · Ski jump	Golfplatz · Sprungschanze
Church · Chapel	Kirche im Ort, freistehend · Kapelle
Monastery · Monastery ruin	Kloster · Klosterruine
Synagogue · Mosque	Synagoge · Moschee
Palace, castle · Ruin	Schloss, Burg · Schloss-, Burgruine
Tower · Radio-, TV-tower	Turm · Funk-, Fernsehturm
Lighthouse · Power station	Leuchtturm · Kraftwerk
Waterfall · Lock	Wasserfall · Schleuse
Important building · Market place, area	Bauwerk · Marktplatz, Areal
Arch. excavation, ruins · Mine	Ausgrabungs- u. Ruinenstätte · Bergwerk
Dolmen · Menhir · Nuraghe	Dolmen · Menhir · Nuraghen
Cairn · Military cemetery	Hünen-, Hügelgrab · Soldatenfriedhof
Hotel, inn, refuge · Cave	Hotel, Gasthaus, Berghütte · Höhle

Datum — Date

Trento

14   E45

Weinstraße   ~1510

Culture
Picturesque town · Elevation — **Kultur** Malerisches Ortsbild · Ortshöhe

WIEN (171)

Worth a journey — Eine Reise wert

★★ **MILANO**

Worth a detour — Lohnt einen Umweg

★ **TEMPLIN**

Worth seeing — Sehenswert

Andermatt

Landscape
Worth a journey — **Landschaft** Eine Reise wert

★★ **Las Cañadas**

Worth a detour — Lohnt einen Umweg

★ **Texel**

Worth seeing — Sehenswert

Dikti

Trips & Tours — **Ausflüge & Touren**

The perfect route — **Perfekte Route**

MARCO POLO Highlight — **MARCO POLO Highlight**

INDEX

This index lists all islands, places and destinations featured in this guide.
Numbers in bold indicate a main entry.

WRITE TO US

e-mail: info@marcopologuides.co.uk

Did you have a great holiday?
Is there something on your mind?
Whatever it is, let us know!
Whether you want to praise, alert us
to errors or give us a personal tip –
MARCO POLO would be pleased to
hear from you.
We do everything we can to provide the
very latest information for your trip.

Nevertheless, despite all of our authors'
thorough research, errors can creep in.
MARCO POLO does not accept any
liability for this. Please contact us by
e-mail or post.

MARCO POLO Travel Publishing Ltd
Pinewood, Chineham Business Park
Crockford Lane, Chineham
Basingstoke, Hampshire RG24 8AL
United Kingdom

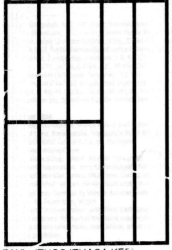

en Schierholz: Karsten Pöllny (16 bottom); DuMont
3, 34, 44/45, 46, 52/53, 56, 59, 68, 70, 98, 101, 125);
16 top); Glowimages: Harding (90/91); R. Hackenberg
28, 38/39, 42, 72, 76, 86); Huber: Giovanni Simeone
); Laif: Caputo (front flap right, 2 top, 4, 100 top), Le
4 (1 top); mauritius images: age (81, 94/95), Bibikow
gebroker (Eisele-Hein) (26 left); Naundorf/Siegmann
Naundorf/Siegmann/Komis Restaurant (27); Okapia/
; Windmill Restaurant: Y. Potamiti (17 bottom)

inewood, Chineham Business Park,
Kingdom. E-mail: sales@marcopolouk.com

elis; Picture editors: Iris Kaczmarczyk, Gabriele Forst
las & pull-out map: © MAIRDUMONT, Ostfildern
cover, page 1: factor product munich
nglish edition: Margaret Howie, fullproof.co.za

H, Stuttgart, Editorial by Pons Wörterbücher
stored in a retrieval system or transmitted in any form
rding or otherwise) without prior written permission

ZAKYNTHOS ITHACA KEF
Zakynthos Ithaca Kefal Lefk
407504/00021 - 1 of 1

DOS & DON'TS 👆

Aa few things you should look out for on your holiday

DO COVER UP IN THE CHURCHES

Greeks are used to seeing some skin in the beach resorts but in the villages you should dress more conservatively. In the churches and monasteries it is expected that knees and shoulders be covered.

DON'T PHOTOGRAPH WITHOUT PERMISSION

Many Greeks love to have their photograph taken, but dislike tourists that act as though they are on safari. Before you just start snapping away, smile at the person you want to photograph and wait for their permission.

DON'T BE SHOCKED BY THE PRICE OF FISH

Fresh fish is very expensive and is often sold by weight. Always ask for the kilo price first and when the fish is being weighed, make sure you are present to avoid any unpleasant surprises.

DO STAY ON SURFACED ROADS

If you are travelling with a hired vehicle and leave the road, you will be driving without insurance and will have to pay for any damages yourself. Tyre and windshield damage is not insured even if the damage occurred on a surfaced road.

DON'T ASK ABOUT THE COMPETITION

Greeks are very honest. But if you go into a taverna and ask about another one you will be told that it doesn't exist, that the owner has passed away or that the police have closed it down.

DON'T TAKE ARTEFACTS OR ANTIQUES

Antiques, old weavings and embroidery as well as old icons may only be exported with special permission. On the beach and in the mountains no one will mind if you collect a pebble or two but taking a stone that has been crafted into something or ceramic shards from an archaeological site is an offence liable for prosecution.

DO BE CAUTIOUS OF THE 'HANDMADE' LABEL

The icons in the souvenir shops are often described as 'handmade'. But it is usually only a silkscreen print done by hand and not a genuinely handmade icon.

DON'T FORGET YOUR HIKING SHOES

Sandals are not even suitable for short hikes; at the very least wear sturdy trainers. The paths are often stony and slippery. And there are snakes – only a few and they are timid – but it is best to be cautious. Long trousers will protect you from thorns.